Better Homes and Gardens®

Wok Cuisine

ORIENTAL TO AMERICAN

©Copyright 1991 by Meredith Corporation, Des Moines, Iowa.
All Rights Reserved. Printed in the United States of America.
First Edition. First Printing.
Library of Congress Catalog Card Number: 90-63298
ISBN: 0-696-01950-7

Our seal assures you that every recipe in *Wok Cuisine* has been tested in the Better Homes and Gardens® Test Kitchen. This means that each recipe is practical and reliable, and meets our high standards of taste appeal. We guarantee your satisfaction with this book for as long as you own it.

WE CARE! ━━━━━━━

All of us at Better Homes and Gardens® Books are dedicated to providing you with the information and ideas you need to create tasty foods. We welcome your comments or suggestions. Write us at: Better Homes and Gardens® Books, Cookbook Editorial Department, LS-348, 1716 Locust Street, Des Moines, Iowa   50336

BETTER HOMES AND GARDENS® BOOKS
Art Director: Ernest Shelton
Managing Editor: David A. Kirchner
Project Editors: James D. Blume, Marsha Jahns
Project Managers: Liz Anderson, Jennifer Speer Ramundt,
  Angela K. Renkoski

Food and Family Life Editor: Sharyl Heiken
Associate Department Editors: Sandra Granseth,
  Rosemary C. Hutchinson, Elizabeth Woolever
Senior Food Editors: Linda Henry, Mary Jo Plutt,
  Joyce Trollope
Associate Food Editors: Jennifer Darling,
  Heather M. Hephner, Shelli McConnell, Heidi McNutt,
  Mary Major Williams
Test Kitchen: Director, Sharon Stilwell; Photo Studio
  Director, Janet Herwig; Home Economists: Lynn
  Blanchard, Kay Cargill, Marilyn Cornelius, Maryellyn
  Krantz, Jennifer Nuese, Colleen Weeden

Associate Art Directors: Neoma Thomas, Linda Ford Vermie,
  Randall Yontz
Assistant Art Directors: Lynda Haupert, Harijs Priekulis,
  Tom Wegner
Graphic Designers: Mary Schlueter Bendgen, Michael Burns,
  Mick Schnepf
Art Production: Director, John Berg; Associate, Joe Heuer;
  Office Manager, Michaela Lester

President, Book Group: Jeramy Landauer
Vice President, Retail Marketing: Jamie L. Martin
Vice President, Administrative Services: Rick Rundall

BETTER HOMES AND GARDENS® MAGAZINE
President, Magazine Group: James A. Autry
Editorial Director: Doris Eby
Food and Nutrition Editor: Nancy Byal

MEREDITH CORPORATION OFFICERS
Chairman of the Executive Committee: E. T. Meredith III
Chairman of the Board: Robert A. Burnett
President and Chief Executive Officer: Jack D. Rehm

WOK CUISINE
Editors: Heather M. Hephner, Shelli McConnell
Graphic Designer: Mary Schlueter Bendgen
Project Managers: Liz Anderson, Jennifer Speer Ramundt
Electronic Text Processor: Paula Forest
Contributing Editor: Marcia Stanley
Food Stylists: Lynn Blanchard, Kathleen E. German,
  Pat Godsted, Janet Herwig
Contributing Photographers: Sean Fitzgerald;
  M. Jensen Photography; Tim Schultz Photography Inc.

On the cover: Sesame Chicken and Vegetables
(see recipe, page 35)

The wok, one of the most versatile pans in the kitchen, is used not only for stir-frying, but also for frying, simmering, and steaming. With this in mind, we loaded **Wok Cuisine** *with a multitude of recipes that you can prepare easily in your wok.*

Start paging through the book and you'll discover versions of classic Oriental dishes, such as Moo Goo Gai Pan and Yang Chow Fried Rice, as well as newly created recipes, such as Plum Delicious Chicken Stir-Fry and Pork and Spinach Salad. To identify recipes that are patterned after classic Oriental dishes, look for a red symbol and the phrase Chinese, Japanese, Korean, Thai, or Vietnamese Specialty.

Besides an array of recipes, you'll also find an assortment of special features. We've included information ranging from a special workshop outlining each cooking technique to a show-and-tell section on cutting meats and vegetables. You'll also find a step-by-step guide for simple garnishing and an illustrated glossary of Oriental ingredients.

Contents

Wok Basics

The earliest woks, invented centuries ago in Asia, were cast-iron pans with sloping sides typically used for stir-frying. Now, available in various styles and materials, woks are used for frying, steaming, and even simmering. In this chapter, you'll discover an assortment of woks and accessories available today.

Electric Wok

Classic Round-Bottom Wok

Flat-Bottom Wok

Stir-Fry Pan

7

THE WOK

Although the same cooking techniques can be performed in all woks, not all woks are the same. Woks vary in size, in shape, in the materials used to make them, and in the accessories packaged with them. With many options to choose from, consider the features that will best suit your cooking needs.

Woks vary in diameter and volume. The most common-size wok, 14 to 16 inches in diameter, is the perfect size for household ranges and accommodates enough food for up to four main-dish servings. Larger woks are cumbersome and generally are used in restaurants. Smaller woks work well on apartment-size stoves and for small meals for two, but they are not large enough for the recipes in this book.

CHOOSING A WOK

When it comes to selecting a wok, there are three things you need to consider.

First, consider the type of range you have. If you have a gas range, choose either a round-bottom or flat-bottom wok. If you have an electric range, however, a flat-bottom wok is the most appropriate. When a round-bottom wok with a ring stand is used on an electric range, the heat that is trapped between the electric heating element and the wok becomes so intense that it can cause discoloration of the range surface. *Or,* if you prefer not to use your range, try a freestanding wok, such as an electric wok (see tip, at right).

Next, think about how much time you want to put into the care of your wok. Steel woks, the most popular kind, need special care before the initial use as well as additional seasoning after each use. On the other hand, aluminum or stainless steel woks need little care and minimal seasoning after each use.

Finally, evaluate how you want your wok to look after several uses. As a steel wok becomes well seasoned, it darkens in color. Aluminum woks may darken too, but can be shined up with an aluminum cleaner. Stainless steel woks remain looking like new, even after several uses.

STYLES OF WOKS

Woks tend to have the same basic shape—a bowl with sloping sides—but there are some differences to consider.

■ A *classic round-bottom wok,* a wok with a ring stand needed to support it, is appropriate for use on a gas range, but is not recommended for an electric range.

For use on a gas range, place the ring stand over the largest burner with the narrow side up. This way the wok is elevated over the hottest part of the flame.

■ A *flat-bottom wok or stir-fry pan,* which is well-suited for electric or gas ranges, is a variation of the classic design. The flat bottom allows the pan to sit directly on the heating element; no ring stand is needed. Even though they look the same and are used in the same manner, a flat-bottom wok is usually sold with a lid, while a stir-fry pan is not. You may purchase lids separately in most cookware shops or Oriental markets.

■ An *electric wok* and portability go hand in hand. With an electric wok, you can cook at the table, the counter, or almost anywhere you wish. However, because the wok's thermostat cycles on and off, the food may take a little longer to cook.

CARING FOR YOUR WOK

Like any cooking appliance or utensil, your wok needs special care for its quality to be maintained. The type of care your wok needs, however, depends on the material of which it is made. Some woks need very little care for their shiny, new looks and original cooking properties to be maintained, but others need more extensive care.

STEEL WOKS

New steel woks come with a rust-resistant coating that must be removed before using. To remove this coating, thoroughly scrub the wok and lid inside and out with a cleanser or scouring pad and hot soapy water. Then, rinse the wok thoroughly with hot water and dry it with a towel. To make sure the wok is completely dry, heat it on your range for a few minutes. Season the wok before using, and reseason after each use (see tip, at right).

ALUMINUM AND STAINLESS STEEL WOKS

Woks made of aluminum or stainless steel require minimum care. Clean them in hot soapy water after each use and use an aluminum or stainless steel cleaner after every few uses. The cleaner helps to keep the outside of the wok looking shiny and new.

Some aluminum and stainless steel woks have interior nonstick coatings that need seasoning. Because the methods for seasoning and cleaning these woks depend on the type of coating, first check the manufacturer's directions. Most nonstick coatings need a thorough cleaning and drying, then a small amount of cooking oil rubbed over the interior surface. Also, you should never scrub a wok's nonstick coating with any type of abrasive. All woks need to be stored in a well-ventilated place.

ELECTRIC WOKS

Follow the manufacturer's directions for cleaning an electric wok. If your wok is immersible for washing, be sure to remove any parts not immersible, such as the heat control. Thoroughly dry every part of the wok before you reassemble it or plug it in.

SEASONING A STEEL WOK

To season a new steel wok, after the rust-resistant coating has been removed, add 2 tablespoons of cooking oil to the wok. Tilt and rotate the wok to evenly coat with oil. Heat the wok over high heat till the wok and oil are very hot. Remove from heat. Allow the wok to cool. Then, using a paper towel, rub in the oil. If the lid also is steel, season it the same way, except remove any nonmetal handles and place the lid directly on a burner of your range.

To clean and reseason your steel wok after each use, soak the wok in hot water (no detergent is necessary or recommended), then clean it well with a bamboo brush or loofah sponge. Rinse thoroughly and dry with a towel. Heat the wok on the range to be sure it is totally dry. Then add about 1 teaspoon of cooking oil to the wok and rub it in with a paper towel. If the lid also is steel, thoroughly clean and dry the lid and rub it with oil.

Avoid putting a seasoned wok in the dishwasher. The harsh detergents and hot water will destroy the seasoning and may cause the wok to rust.

Store your seasoned wok in a well-ventilated place. Long periods in a warm, airless cupboard can cause the oil used in seasoning to become rancid.

Steamer Rack

Bamboo
Brush

Spatula

Wire-Mesh
Strainer

Deep-Fat Frying
Thermometer

Wok Rack

Tongs

Chopsticks

WOK ACCESSORIES

Just as there are a variety of woks, there are numerous accessories that often come with woks or can be purchased separately.

The accessories below can help make using your wok easier, whether you are stir-frying, frying, simmering, or steaming.

SPATULA
An essential tool for stir-frying is a long-handled utensil used for keeping the food in motion over the heat. A Chinese spatula has a wide, slightly curved metal blade that is perfect for the job. Another option is a wooden spoon or spatula. To avoid damaging the nonstick surface of the wok, use a wooden spoon or spatula.

DEEP-FAT FRYING THERMOMETER
The temperature of the fat is the single most important factor in successful deep-fat frying, and a thermometer helps you monitor it. However, not all deep-fat frying thermometers are suited for use in woks. Choose a thermometer that is long enough to clip on the side of the wok, but made so the bulb doesn't touch the wok's edge.

STEAMER RACK
Steamer racks are made from many different materials and are available in a variety of styles and sizes. The purpose of a steamer rack, and what makes it essential for steaming, is that it holds food over simmering water, allowing steam to surround and cook it.

Classic bamboo steamer racks can be stacked to cook several foods at the same time. These racks have their own snug lids, so you don't need to use the wok lid. Other steamer racks, including the kinds most commonly packaged with woks, are simply flat, metal rounds that settle part way down the wok's sides. See "The Steaming Workshop" on page 116 for ways you can make your own steaming rack.

WOK RACK
This semicircular or doughnut-shape wire rack hangs from the sides of a wok. Use it when you deep-fat fry to drain the food and keep it warm. The advantage of this rack is that excess oil drains off the food and returns to the wok.

WIRE-MESH STRAINER
When frying in hot oil, a wire-mesh strainer is perfect for removing the cooked food from the hot oil. The wire mesh allows the oil to drip off the food, and the wooden handle helps protect your hand from intense heat. If you don't have a wire strainer, use a long-handled slotted spoon.

CHOPSTICKS
Commonly used as eating utensils, chopsticks also are used in Oriental kitchens for stirring and cooking. Use bamboo or wooden chopsticks in food preparation.

TONGS
Whether they're the wooden ones sometimes packaged with a wok or the metal ones found in most household kitchens, tongs are useful for removing fried foods from hot oil or steamed foods from the steamer rack.

BAMBOO BRUSH
A bamboo brush, known as a gentle Oriental scouring pad, is the perfect utensil for cleaning your wok. But if you don't have one, use a loofah sponge or a nylon or plastic scrubber instead. Don't use any abrasive pad or cleaner that could damage nonstick or seasoned surfaces.

Stir-Frying

Traditionally an Oriental cooking technique, stir-frying has been adopted and adapted by American cooks. Here is a collection of favorite Oriental classics, as well as dozens of delectable, newly created stir-fry recipes.

12   *Phoenix and Dragon*
(see recipe, page 54)

Stir-frying is a quick and easy cooking process that results in delicious and fresh-tasting foods. To make sure everything goes smoothly, take a look at the helpful hints in "The Stir-Frying Workshop" before you begin.

THE STIR-FRYING WORKSHOP

As the name implies, stir-frying is a cooking method that involves stirring and frying food at the same time. The food is lifted and turned as it cooks quickly in just enough oil to prevent sticking.

Cooking food fast is the key to good stir-frying. Cutting the food into small, thin pieces and cooking small amounts at one time make the quick cooking possible. When cooked quickly, vegetables keep their crispness and color, and meats stay tender and juicy.

EQUIPMENT FOR STIR-FRYING

■ The sloping sides and large surface area of a wok make it easy to lift and turn the food to keep it in motion. However, if you don't have a wok, a large skillet (10 inches in diameter) will work just as well.

■ A long-handled spatula or wooden spoon is indispensable when it comes to stir-frying. This utensil allows you to lift and turn the food without your hands getting too hot or burned.

GUIDES TO GOOD STIR-FRYING

1. It's important to have all of the ingredients ready to go before you begin stir-frying. You'll find that once you start, cooking goes too quickly for you to prepare ingredients between cooking steps.

Start by slicing all of the ingredients, combining the sauce ingredients, and cooking the rice or pasta called for in the recipe. Arrange all of the ingredients in dishes near the wok so you can reach them easily when it's time to use them.

2. When everything is ready, add the cooking oil to a wok or large skillet. Lift and tilt the wok to evenly distribute the oil over the bottom. Preheat the wok over medium-high heat about 1 minute.

To test the hotness of the oil, add a single piece of vegetable to the hot wok. If it sizzles, proceed with cooking the seasonings, vegetables, and meats as directed in the recipe. You may need to add additional oil during stir-frying to prevent the food from sticking. The amount of oil needed for stir-frying depends on the wok's surface. For example, a wok with a nonstick surface probably will need less oil than a wok with a steel surface. If you need to add more cooking oil, add a small amount at a time, and bring the oil to frying temperature before proceeding.

3. Seasonings, such as minced garlic and grated gingerroot, generally are stir-fried first for 15 seconds so the distinctive flavor of the ingredient seasons the oil.

Just stir the seasoning into the hot oil, keeping it in constant motion. Because the amount you will be stir-frying at one time is so small, it's important to keep the seasoning moving the entire time so it does not burn.

4. Now you're ready to stir-fry the vegetables. Begin by stir-frying the vegetables that take the longest to cook, then follow with those that cook more quickly. Use a long-handled spatula or wooden spoon to gently lift and turn the pieces of food with a folding motion, as shown below. This ensures that the food will cook evenly.

To prevent scorching, remember to keep the food moving at all times. Remove the vegetables from the wok after stir-frying.

5. Next, stir-fry the meat, poultry, or fish. Since overloading the wok or skillet with food will slow cooking, stir-fry no more than 12 ounces of meat at one time.

This means that for most recipes, you'll begin by stir-frying only *half* of the meat until it is done, and then remove it from the wok. Then, you'll stir-fry the remaining *half* of the meat. Return all of the cooked meat to the wok.

6. To thicken the sauce, push the cooked meat from the center of the wok. If the sauce ingredients you've already mixed together contain cornstarch, you'll need to restir. Then, pour the sauce mixture into the center of the wok and cook, stirring constantly, till it thickens and bubbles over the entire surface, as shown below.

7. The final step of stir-frying is to return all of the stir-fried ingredients to the center of the wok. Stir everything together to coat with the sauce. Then, cook and stir the mixture as directed in the recipe until heated through.
To assure that your stir-fry is piping hot, serve immediately.

BEEF AND FRIED POTATO STIR-FRY

VIETNAMESE SPECIALTY

This dish containing white potatoes is an example of the French influence on Vietnamese cooking. The French introduced the white potato to Vietnam more than 100 years ago.

12 ounces beef top round steak
½ cup water
3 tablespoons fish sauce
1 tablespoon cornstarch
¼ teaspoon pepper
2 medium potatoes (10 ounces total) or 2 cups frozen french-fried shoestring potatoes, thawed
1 tablespoon cooking oil

2 cloves garlic, minced
1 medium onion, cut into thin wedges (¾ cup)
1 medium green pepper, cut into 1-inch pieces (1 cup)
2 medium tomatoes, cut into thin wedges (2½ cups)
Cilantro or parsley sprigs (optional)

■ Trim fat from beef. Partially freeze beef. Thinly slice across the grain into bite-size strips. For sauce, in a small bowl stir together the water, fish sauce, cornstarch, and pepper. Set aside.

■ If using fresh potatoes, peel potatoes and cut into julienne strips. Rinse the potato strips. Pat the fresh potato strips or thawed shoestring potatoes dry with paper towels. Pour cooking oil into a wok or 12-inch skillet. (Add more oil as necessary during cooking.) Preheat over medium-high heat. Stir-fry garlic in hot oil for 15 seconds. Add the potatoes. If using fresh potatoes, stir-fry about 6 minutes or till tender. If using shoestring potatoes, stir-fry for 2 to 3 minutes or till golden. Remove potatoes from the wok. Add the onion to the wok; stir-fry for 1 minute. Add the green pepper and stir-fry about 2 minutes more or till vegetables are crisp-tender. Remove the vegetables from the wok.

■ Add the beef to the hot wok. Stir-fry for 2 to 3 minutes or to desired doneness. Push beef from the center of the wok. Stir sauce. Add the sauce to the center of the wok. Cook and stir till thickened and bubbly.

■ Return the cooked vegetables to the wok. Stir all ingredients together to coat with sauce. Cook and stir about 1 minute more or till heated through. Gently stir in the tomato wedges. Heat through. Serve immediately. If desired, garnish with cilantro or parsley. Makes 4 servings.

Nutrition information per serving: 252 calories, 22 g protein, 23 g carbohydrate, 9 g fat (2 g saturated), 52 mg cholesterol, 970 mg sodium, 725 mg potassium.

VEGETABLE-BEEF STIR-FRY

12 ounces boneless beef sirloin
    or top round steak
⅓ cup soy sauce
¼ cup water
2 green onions, thinly sliced
    (¼ cup)
2 cloves garlic, minced
1 tablespoon sugar
2 teaspoons sesame oil
1 teaspoon sesame seed, crushed
¼ teaspoon pepper

4 dried mushrooms
2 ounces bean threads
1 tablespoon cooking oil
2 medium carrots, cut into
    julienne strips (1 cup)
1 medium onion, cut into thin
    wedges (¾ cup)
1 8-ounce can bamboo shoots,
    drained
1½ cups shredded Chinese
    cabbage or spinach

KOREAN SPECIALTY
Vegetable-Beef Stir-Fry, called "chap-chee" in Korean, is a classic family dish. Most Korean cooks have their own version of the recipe, but they typically combine spicy marinated beef strips with a variety of thinly sliced fresh vegetables.

炒
鍋
烹
飪

■ Trim fat from beef. Partially freeze beef. Thinly slice across the grain into matchstick-size shreds. For marinade, in a large mixing bowl stir together the soy sauce, water, green onions, garlic, sugar, sesame oil, sesame seed, and pepper. Stir in the beef. Cover and marinate at room temperature for 30 minutes or in the refrigerator for 2 hours, stirring occasionally.

■ Meanwhile, in a small mixing bowl soak the dried mushrooms for 30 minutes in enough warm water to cover. Rinse well and squeeze to drain thoroughly. Slice thinly, discarding stems. In a medium mixing bowl soak the bean threads for 15 minutes in enough warm water to cover. Drain well. Squeeze out excess moisture. Cut bean threads into 4-inch lengths. Set aside. Drain the meat, reserving marinade.

■ Pour the cooking oil into a wok or large skillet. (Add more oil as necessary during cooking.) Preheat over medium-high heat. Add the carrots and stir-fry for 2 minutes. Add the onion; stir-fry for 3 minutes. Add the bamboo shoots and mushrooms; stir-fry about 1 minute more or till vegetables are crisp-tender. Remove the vegetables from the wok.

■ Add beef to the hot wok. Stir-fry 2 to 3 minutes or to desired doneness. Stir the reserved marinade, bean threads, cooked vegetables, and Chinese cabbage or spinach into the wok. Cook and stir 1 minute more or till heated through and juices are absorbed. Serve immediately. Makes 4 servings.

Nutrition information per serving: 311 calories, 26 g protein, 26 g carbohydrate, 12 g fat (3 g saturated), 49 mg cholesterol, 1,423 mg sodium, 789 mg potassium.

Beef and Tomatoes over Noodles

BEEF AND TOMATOES OVER NOODLES

12 ounces beef top round steak
⅔ cup beef broth
¼ cup soy sauce
2 tablespoons cornstarch
2 teaspoons vinegar
1 teaspoon sugar
⅛ to ¼ teaspoon ground red
    pepper
8 Individual Noodle Cakes
    (see recipe, page 87)
1 tablespoon cooking oil

2 cloves garlic, minced
2 medium green peppers, cut
    into julienne strips (2 cups)
1 medium onion, cut into thin
    wedges (¾ cup)
2 medium tomatoes, cut into
    thin wedges (2½ cups)
    Tomato Roses (see directions,
    page 199) (optional)
    Chives (optional)

This saucy beef and tomato mixture is also delicious served over hot cooked rice or fine egg noodles instead of the noodle cakes.

■ Trim fat from beef. Partially freeze beef. Thinly slice across the grain into bite-size strips. For sauce, in a small bowl stir together the beef broth, soy sauce, cornstarch, vinegar, sugar, and ground red pepper. Set aside.

■ Prepare the noodle cakes. Keep warm.

■ Pour cooking oil into a wok or large skillet. (Add more oil as necessary during cooking.) Preheat over medium-high heat. Stir-fry garlic in hot oil for 15 seconds. Add green peppers and onion; stir-fry about 2 minutes or till vegetables are crisp-tender. Remove the vegetables from the wok.

■ Add the beef to the hot wok. Stir-fry for 2 to 3 minutes or to desired doneness. Push beef from the center of the wok.

■ Stir sauce. Add the sauce to the center of the wok. Cook and stir till thickened and bubbly. Return the cooked vegetables to the wok; add tomato wedges. Stir all ingredients together to coat with sauce. Cover and cook for 1 minute more. To serve, slide 2 noodle cakes onto each plate. Spoon beef mixture over noodles. Serve immediately. If desired, garnish with Tomato Roses and chives. Makes 4 servings.

Nutrition information per serving: 392 calories, 25 g protein, 36 g carbohydrate, 17 g fat (3 g saturated), 79 mg cholesterol, 1,215 mg sodium, 606 mg potassium.

Sunburst Stir-Fry

This zesty dish gets its name from the colorful red pepper and yellow summer squash.

1 pound boneless beef sirloin steak
1 large sweet red pepper, cut up (1⅓ cups)
2 tablespoons soy sauce
½ teaspoon crushed red pepper
¼ teaspoon pepper
1 tablespoon cooking oil
2 cloves garlic, minced

2 medium yellow summer squash, halved lengthwise and sliced ¼ inch thick (2½ cups)
1 medium onion, cut into thin wedges (¾ cup)
3 cups hot cooked rice
Green onion slivers or Onion Brushes (see directions, page 198) (optional)

■ Trim fat from beef. Partially freeze beef. Thinly slice across the grain into bite-size strips. Set aside.

■ In a blender container or food processor bowl place the sweet red pepper. Cover and blend or process till ground. For sauce, in a small bowl stir together the soy sauce, crushed red pepper, and pepper. Set aside.

■ Pour cooking oil into a wok or large skillet. (Add more oil as necessary during cooking.) Preheat over medium-high heat. Stir-fry garlic in hot oil for 15 seconds. Add squash and onion; stir-fry about 3 minutes or till vegetables are crisp-tender. Remove the vegetables from the wok.

■ Add *half* of the beef to the hot wok. Stir-fry for 2 to 3 minutes or to desired doneness. Remove beef from wok. Repeat with the remaining beef. Return all beef to the wok.

■ Return the cooked vegetables to the wok. Add the ground sweet red pepper and the sauce. Stir all ingredients together to coat with sauce. Cook and stir about 1 minute more or till heated through. Serve immediately over hot cooked rice. If desired, garnish with green onion slivers or Onion Brushes. Makes 4 servings.

Nutrition information per serving: 443 calories, 30 g protein, 52 g carbohydrate, 12 g fat (4 g saturated), 65 mg cholesterol, 578 mg sodium, 701 mg potassium.

SZECHWAN BEEF

1 pound beef top round steak
6 dried mushrooms
3 medium carrots, roll cut
    (2 cups)
¼ cup hot bean sauce
3 tablespoons dry sherry
2 tablespoons soy sauce
¾ teaspoon whole Szechwan
    peppers, crushed, or whole
    black peppers, crushed

1 tablespoon cooking oil
½ teaspoon purchased chili oil
    or Chili Oil (see recipe,
    page 82)
1 clove garlic, minced
3 stalks celery, thinly bias sliced
    (1½ cups)
3 cups hot cooked Chinese egg
    noodles

**CHINESE
SPECIALTY**
*Chili oil, a spicy red-
colored oil seasoned
by chili peppers, gives
this Szechwan dish
its hotness.*

■ Trim fat from beef. Partially freeze beef. Thinly slice across the grain into bite-size strips. In a small mixing bowl soak the mushrooms for 30 minutes in enough warm water to cover. Rinse well and squeeze to drain thoroughly. Slice thinly, discarding stems. Set aside.

■ Meanwhile, in a medium saucepan cook carrots, covered, in a small amount of boiling water for 3½ minutes. Drain and set aside. For sauce, in a small bowl stir together the bean sauce, sherry, soy sauce, and crushed Szechwan pepper or black pepper. Set aside.

■ Pour cooking oil and chili oil into a wok or large skillet. (Add more cooking oil as necessary during cooking.) Preheat over medium-high heat. Stir-fry garlic in hot oil for 15 seconds. Add celery; stir-fry for 2 minutes. Add the mushrooms and carrots; stir-fry for 1 to 2 minutes more or till vegetables are crisp-tender. Remove the vegetables from the wok.

■ Add *half* of the beef to the hot wok. Stir-fry for 2 to 3 minutes or to desired doneness. Remove beef from wok. Repeat with the remaining beef. Return all beef to the wok. Stir sauce. Add the sauce to the wok.

■ Return the cooked vegetables to the wok. Stir all ingredients together to coat with sauce. Cook and stir about 1 minute more or till heated through. Serve immediately over hot cooked Chinese egg noodles. Makes 4 servings.

Nutrition information per serving: 440 calories, 34 g protein, 45 g carbohydrate, 13 g fat (3 g saturated), 107 mg cholesterol, 1,226 mg sodium, 819 mg potassium.

*To soak dried
mushrooms, place the
mushrooms in a small
bowl with enough
warm water to cover
and soak them for 30
minutes to soften.
Rinse well and squeeze
to drain thoroughly.
Thinly slice the
mushrooms, discarding
the tough stems.*

MONGOLIAN BEEF

*Although this is not an authentic recipe of Mongolia, the popular dish is given the name by Chinese-American restaurants. It's called **Mongolian Beef** because the wine, garlic, and onions used in the recipe are typically used by the Mongols.*

1 pound beef flank steak **or** boneless beef round steak
⅓ cup water
2 tablespoons rice wine **or** dry white wine
1 tablespoon hoisin sauce
1 tablespoon hot bean sauce **or** ½ teaspoon ground red pepper
1 tablespoon soy sauce

2 teaspoons cornstarch
1 teaspoon sesame oil (optional)
1 tablespoon cooking oil
2 cloves garlic, minced
10 to 12 green onions, bias sliced into 1-inch lengths (2 cups)
Fried Rice Sticks (see recipe, page 86) **or** 3 cups hot cooked rice

■ Trim fat from beef. Partially freeze beef. Thinly slice across the grain into bite-size strips. For sauce, in a small bowl stir together the water, rice wine or dry white wine, hoisin sauce, bean sauce or ground red pepper, soy sauce, cornstarch, and, if desired, sesame oil. Set aside.

■ Pour cooking oil into a wok or large skillet. (Add more oil as necessary during cooking.) Preheat over medium-high heat. Stir-fry garlic in hot oil for 15 seconds. Add green onions and stir-fry about 1½ minutes or till onions are tender. Remove onions from the wok.

■ Add *half* of the beef to the hot wok. Stir-fry for 2 to 3 minutes or to desired doneness. Remove beef from wok. Repeat with the remaining beef. Return all beef to the wok. Push beef from the center of the wok. Stir sauce. Add sauce to the center of the wok. Cook and stir till thickened and bubbly.

■ Return the onions to the wok. Stir all ingredients together to coat with sauce. Cook and stir about 1 minute more or till heated through. Serve immediately over Fried Rice Sticks or hot cooked rice. Makes 4 servings.

Nutrition information per serving: 443 calories, 26 g protein, 30 g carbohydrate, 23 g fat (7 g saturated), 60 mg cholesterol, 575 mg sodium, 552 mg potassium.

GROUND BEEF SALAD

¼ cup water
¼ cup fish sauce
3 tablespoons lemon or lime juice
½ to 1 teaspoon crushed red pepper
1 tablespoon cooking oil
2 cloves garlic, minced
2 green onions, bias sliced into 1-inch lengths (⅓ cup)

1 pound lean ground beef
8 cups torn mixed greens
1 medium cucumber, thinly sliced (1¾ cups)
2 medium tomatoes, cut into wedges (1½ cups)
2 small carrots, thinly bias sliced (⅔ cup)

THAI SPECIALTY
Here's a recipe that's perfect for using garden produce. If you'd like, substitute broccoli, cauliflower, or radishes for the cucumber, tomatoes, and carrots in this dish.

■ For sauce, in a small bowl stir together the water, fish sauce, lemon or lime juice, and crushed red pepper. Set aside.

■ Pour cooking oil into a wok or large skillet. (Add more oil as necessary during cooking.) Preheat over medium-high heat. Stir-fry garlic in hot oil for 15 seconds. Add green onions; stir-fry about 1½ minutes or till onions are tender. Remove onions from wok.

■ Break up the ground beef. Add *half* of the beef to the hot wok. Stir-fry for 2 to 3 minutes or till brown. Remove the beef from the wok. Drain off fat. Repeat with remaining beef. Return all beef to the wok. Add the sauce to the wok. Stir ingredients together to coat with sauce. Cook and stir for 2 minutes to blend flavors. Stir in the green onions. Cook and stir about 1 minute more or till heated through.

■ Divide the mixed greens among 4 plates. Spoon the ground beef mixture atop the greens. Arrange the cucumber slices, tomato wedges, and carrot slices around the beef mixture. Makes 4 servings.

Nutrition information per serving: 325 calories, 30 g protein, 12 g carbohydrate, 18 g fat (6 g saturated), 84 mg cholesterol, 1,306 mg sodium, 896 mg potassium.

STIR-FRIED PORK AND VEGETABLES

1 pound lean boneless pork
1 8-ounce package frozen whole baby sweet corn, thawed, **or** one 15-ounce can whole baby sweet corn, drained
½ cup water
2 tablespoons soy sauce
2 tablespoons dry sherry
4 teaspoons cornstarch
½ teaspoon instant chicken bouillon granules
1 tablespoon cooking oil
2 cloves garlic, minced

3 medium carrots, thinly bias sliced (1½ cups)
2 cups fresh pea pods **or** one 6-ounce package frozen pea pods, thawed
4 ounces fresh shiitake **or** other fresh mushrooms, sliced (1½ cups)
1 cup jicama cut into julienne strips
3 cups hot cooked rice
Sweet pepper strips (optional)
Parsley sprigs (optional)

■ Trim fat from pork. Partially freeze pork. Thinly slice across the grain into bite-size strips. Halve corn crosswise. For sauce, stir together the water, soy sauce, sherry, cornstarch, and chicken bouillon granules. Set aside.

■ Pour cooking oil into a wok or large skillet. (Add more oil as necessary during cooking.) Preheat over medium-high heat. Stir-fry garlic in hot oil for 15 seconds. Add carrots; stir-fry for 3 minutes. Add fresh pea pods (if using), mushrooms, and baby corn. Stir-fry for 1 to 2 minutes or till vegetables are crisp-tender. Remove the vegetables from the wok.

■ Add *half* of the pork to the hot wok. Stir-fry for 2 to 3 minutes or till no pink remains. Remove pork from wok. Repeat with remaining pork. Return all pork to the wok. Push pork from the center of the wok. Stir sauce. Add sauce to the center of the wok. Cook and stir till thickened and bubbly.

■ Return the cooked vegetables to the wok. Add frozen pea pods (if using) and jicama. Stir all ingredients together to coat with sauce. Cook and stir about 1 minute more or till heated through. Serve immediately with hot cooked rice. If desired, garnish with pepper strips and parsley sprigs. Makes 4 servings.

Nutrition information per serving: 556 calories, 33 g protein, 67 g carbohydrate, 16 g fat (5 g saturated), 77 mg cholesterol, 722 mg sodium, 805 mg potassium.

Stir-Fried Pork and Vegetables

PORK CHOP SUEY

1 pound lean boneless pork
½ cup water
3 tablespoons soy sauce
4 teaspoons cornstarch
1 teaspoon sugar
1 teaspoon instant chicken
   bouillon granules
1 tablespoon cooking oil
2 medium carrots, thinly bias
   sliced (1 cup)
1 stalk celery, thinly bias sliced
   (½ cup)

2 cups fresh bean sprouts or one
   16-ounce can bean sprouts,
   drained
1 cup sliced fresh mushrooms
   or one 4-ounce can sliced
   mushrooms, drained
1 8-ounce can bamboo shoots,
   drained
3 green onions, bias sliced into
   1-inch lengths (about
   ½ cup)
3 cups warmed chow mein
   noodles or hot cooked rice

■ Trim fat from pork. Partially freeze pork. Thinly slice across the grain into bite-size strips. For sauce, in a small bowl stir together the water, soy sauce, cornstarch, sugar, and chicken bouillon granules. Set aside.

■ Pour cooking oil into a wok or 12-inch skillet. (Add more oil as necessary during cooking.) Preheat over medium-high heat. Stir-fry the carrots and celery in hot oil for 2 minutes. Add fresh bean sprouts (if using), fresh mushrooms (if using), bamboo shoots, and green onions. Stir-fry for 1 to 2 minutes more or till carrots and celery are crisp-tender. Remove vegetables.

■ Add *half* of the pork to the hot wok. Stir-fry for 2 to 3 minutes or till no pink remains. Remove pork from wok. Repeat with remaining pork. Return all pork to the wok. Push pork from the center of the wok. Stir sauce. Add the sauce to the center of the wok. Cook and stir till thickened and bubbly.

■ Return cooked vegetables to the wok. Add canned bean sprouts (if using) and canned mushrooms (if using). Stir all ingredients together to coat with sauce. Cook and stir about 1 minute more or till heated through. Serve immediately over chow mein noodles or hot cooked rice. Makes 4 servings.

Nutrition information per serving: 465 calories, 28 g protein, 34 g carbohydrate, 25 g fat (6 g saturated), 71 mg cholesterol, 1,229 mg sodium, 712 mg potassium.

FRUIT 'N' PORK STIR-FRY

1 pound lean boneless pork
1 8-ounce can pineapple chunks
   (juice pack)
½ teaspoon finely shredded
   orange peel
⅓ cup orange juice
2 tablespoons soy sauce
1 tablespoon cornstarch
1 tablespoon cooking oil

1 teaspoon grated gingerroot
1 medium apple, cored and
   coarsely chopped (1 cup)
1 11-ounce can mandarin
   orange sections, drained
¼ cup sliced almonds, toasted
2⅔ cups hot cooked couscous
   or 3 cups hot cooked rice

Fresh gingerroot, a staple in Chinese kitchens, is available in most supermarkets. But if you can't find it, just substitute ¼ teaspoon ground ginger for the gingerroot in this sauce.

■ Trim fat from pork. Partially freeze pork. Thinly slice across the grain into bite-size strips. Drain pineapple, reserving juice. If necessary, add enough *water* to the juice to make ⅓ cup liquid. For sauce, stir together the reserved pineapple juice, orange peel and juice, soy sauce, and cornstarch. Set aside.

■ Pour oil into a wok or large skillet. (Add more oil as necessary during cooking.) Preheat over medium-high heat. Stir-fry gingerroot in hot oil for 15 seconds. Add *half* of the pork to the hot wok. Stir-fry for 2 to 3 minutes or till no pink remains. Remove. Repeat with remaining pork. Return all pork to the wok. Push pork from the center. Stir sauce. Add sauce to the center. Cook and stir till thickened and bubbly. Add pineapple and apple. Stir all ingredients to coat with sauce. Cover; cook for 2 minutes. Stir in mandarin oranges. Sprinkle almonds atop. Serve over couscous or rice. Serves 4.

Nutrition information per serving: 425 calories, 25 g protein, 43 g carbohydrate, 18 g fat (5 g saturated), 71 mg cholesterol, 577 mg sodium, 561 mg potassium.

HANDLING HOT PEPPERS

When a recipe calls for chili peppers, choose them according to the hotness level you want. Generally, the smaller the pepper, the hotter it is. Take a few precautions when handling hot peppers to avoid burning your eyes or skin. Protect your hands by covering them with plastic bags or plastic or rubber gloves. Cook chili peppers just for the time indicated in recipes and avoid breathing directly over the wok as you stir-fry because of the powerful fumes.

MOO SHU PORK

CHINESE SPECIALTY

Moo Shu Pork is typically served tucked inside thin and delicate Mandarin pancakes. To simplify preparation, we used purchased flour tortillas instead.

1 pound lean boneless pork
8 dried mushrooms
8 7- or 8-inch flour tortillas, warmed (see tip, page 159)
2 tablespoons cooking oil
2 beaten eggs
2 teaspoons grated gingerroot
6 green onions, bias sliced into 1-inch lengths (about 1 cup)

½ of an 8-ounce can bamboo shoots, drained
¼ cup hoisin sauce
⅛ teaspoon pepper
⅓ cup purchased plum sauce or *Plum Sauce* (see recipe, page 82)

To serve, brush plum sauce over the tortillas. Then, spoon about ½ cup of the pork filling into the center of each tortilla. To fold the tortillas pocket-style, bring one edge of the tortilla up to overlap the filling. Then, fold the two adjacent edges of the tortilla over the filling.

■ Trim fat from pork. Partially freeze pork. Thinly slice across the grain into bite-size strips. In a small bowl soak mushrooms for 30 minutes in enough warm water to cover. Rinse well and squeeze to drain thoroughly. Chop mushrooms, discarding stems. Set aside. Stack tortillas and wrap tightly in foil. Heat in a 350° oven for 10 minutes to soften.

■ Meanwhile, pour *1 tablespoon* of the cooking oil into a wok or large skillet. Preheat over medium heat. Add eggs. Lift and tilt wok to form a thin sheet of egg. Cook, without stirring, about 2 minutes or just till set. Slide egg sheet onto a cutting board. Thinly slice into bite-size strips. Set aside. Pour the remaining cooking oil into the wok or skillet. (Add more oil as necessary during cooking.) Preheat over medium-high heat. Stir-fry gingerroot in hot oil for 15 seconds. Add green onions; stir-fry about 1½ minutes or till onions are crisp-tender. Remove onions from the wok.

■ Add *half* of the pork to the hot wok. Stir-fry for 2 to 3 minutes or till no pink remains. Remove pork from wok. Repeat with remaining pork. Return all pork to the wok. Add the mushrooms, onions, bamboo shoots, hoisin sauce, and pepper. Stir all ingredients together to coat with hoisin sauce. Cook and stir about 1 minute or till heated through. Stir in the egg strips.

■ To serve, brush some plum sauce over a tortilla. Then, spoon about ½ *cup* of the pork mixture into the center of the tortilla. Fold pocket-style or roll up jelly-roll style. Repeat with remaining tortillas, plum sauce, and pork mixture. Serve immediately. Makes 4 servings.

Nutrition information per serving: 623 calories, 32 g protein, 68 g carbohydrate, 26 g fat (6 g saturated), 177 mg cholesterol, 1,038 mg sodium, 661 mg potassium.

OYSTER-SAUCED PORK 'N' BROCCOLI

1 pound lean boneless pork
½ cup chicken broth
¼ cup oyster sauce
2 teaspoons cornstarch
1 teaspoon sugar
1 tablespoon cooking oil

1 clove garlic, minced
1 teaspoon grated gingerroot
3 cups broccoli flowerets
3 cups hot cooked rice or Fried
    Bean Threads (see recipe,
    page 86)

■ Trim fat from pork. Partially freeze pork. Thinly slice across the grain into bite-size strips. For sauce, stir together the chicken broth, oyster sauce, cornstarch, and sugar. Set aside. Pour cooking oil into a wok or large skillet. (Add more oil as necessary during cooking.) Preheat over medium-high heat. Stir-fry garlic and gingerroot in hot oil for 15 seconds. Add broccoli; stir-fry for 3 to 4 minutes or till crisp-tender. Remove the broccoli.

■ Add *half* of the pork to the hot wok. Stir-fry for 2 to 3 minutes or till no pink remains. Remove pork. Repeat with remaining pork. Return all pork to the wok. Push pork from the center. Stir sauce. Add sauce to the center. Cook and stir till thickened and bubbly. Return broccoli to the wok. Stir all ingredients to coat with sauce. Cook and stir about 1 minute or till heated through. Serve immediately with rice or Fried Bean Threads. Serves 4.

Nutrition information per serving: 458 calories, 28 g protein, 53 g carbohydrate, 15 g fat (4 g saturated), 71 mg cholesterol, 1,019 mg sodium, 608 mg potassium.

CHINESE SPECIALTY
The flavor of oyster sauce is hard to describe, but it is distinctive. Rather than having a definite oyster flavor, it is smooth and mellow and seems to round out the flavors in a dish.

炒
鍋
烹
飪

USING TOFU IN STIR-FRIES

Tofu or bean curd, with its high protein content and smooth texture, is especially popular in Oriental dishes as a meat substitute or extender. You usually can buy soft- or firm-style tofu in shelf-stable boxes in the Oriental food section of your supermarket. Tofu also can be found in the produce section. For stir-fries, choose firm tofu, which holds its shape better for slicing and cubing. To prepare tofu for stir-fried dishes, drain it and cut it into bite-size cubes.
To keep tofu from breaking up in stir-fries, add it at the end of stir-frying and gently stir it into the other ingredients.

SPICY LAMB AND LEEKS

CHINESE SPECIALTY

The mild onion flavor of leeks contrasts with the spiciness of this dish. A leek resembles an oversize green onion with its overlapping, wide, green leaves, fat white stalk, and shaggy roots at the bulb end.

1 pound lean boneless lamb
2 tablespoons soy sauce
1 tablespoon rice wine or dry white wine
1 tablespoon water
2 teaspoons grated gingerroot
1 teaspoon cornstarch
1 teaspoon sugar
½ teaspoon sesame oil or cooking oil
2 tablespoons soy sauce

2 tablespoons rice wine or dry white wine
1 tablespoon hot bean sauce
1 teaspoon sugar
1 tablespoon cooking oil
2 cloves garlic, minced
2 medium leeks, cut into 2-inch-long slivers (about ⅔ cup)
3 cups hot cooked rice

■ Trim fat from lamb. Partially freeze lamb. Thinly slice across the grain into bite-size strips. For marinade, in a large mixing bowl stir together 2 tablespoons soy sauce, the 1 tablespoon rice wine or dry white wine, the water, gingerroot, cornstarch, 1 teaspoon sugar, and the ½ teaspoon sesame oil or cooking oil. Add the lamb; toss to coat. Cover and marinate at room temperature for 30 minutes, stirring occasionally.

■ Meanwhile, for sauce, stir together 2 tablespoons soy sauce, the 2 tablespoons rice wine or dry white wine, hot bean sauce, and 1 teaspoon sugar.

■ Drain lamb, reserving marinade. Pour the 1 tablespoon cooking oil into a wok or large skillet. (Add more oil as necessary during cooking.) Preheat over medium-high heat. Stir-fry garlic in hot oil for 15 seconds. Add leeks and stir-fry about 1 minute or till leeks are tender. Remove leeks.

■ Add *half* of the lamb to the hot wok. Stir-fry for 2 to 3 minutes or to desired doneness. Remove the lamb from the wok. Repeat with remaining lamb. Return all the lamb to the wok. Push lamb from the center of the wok. Stir together the sauce and the reserved marinade, then add to the center of the wok. Cook and stir till thickened and bubbly.

■ Return the leeks to the wok. Stir all ingredients together to coat with sauce. Cook and stir about 1 minute more or till heated through. Serve immediately with hot cooked rice. Makes 4 servings.

Nutrition information per serving: 431 calories, 27 g protein, 51 g carbohydrate, 11 g fat (3 g saturated), 68 mg cholesterol, 1,236 mg sodium, 412 mg potassium.

GLAZED LAMB AND ASPARAGUS

1 pound lean boneless lamb
½ cup water
2 tablespoons hoisin sauce
2 teaspoons cornstarch
1 teaspoon instant chicken
   bouillon granules
1 tablespoon cooking oil
2 teaspoons grated gingerroot
1 pound fresh asparagus, cut
   into 1-inch pieces (3 cups),
   or one 10-ounce package
   frozen cut asparagus,
   thawed

2 green onions, sliced (¼ cup)
¼ cup pine nuts or sliced
   almonds
1 teaspoon finely shredded
   lemon peel
2⅔ cups hot cooked couscous
   or 3 cups hot cooked rice

The lemon and nuts in the sauce give this dish a unique flavor twist and an unexpected crunch.

■ Trim fat from lamb. Partially freeze lamb. Thinly slice across the grain into bite-size strips. For sauce, in a small bowl stir together the water, hoisin sauce, cornstarch, and chicken bouillon granules. Set aside.

■ Pour the cooking oil into a wok or large skillet. (Add more oil as necessary during cooking.) Preheat over medium-high heat. Stir-fry gingerroot in hot oil for 15 seconds. Add the asparagus; stir-fry fresh asparagus for 3 minutes or thawed asparagus for 1½ minutes. Add the green onions; stir-fry about 1½ minutes more or till asparagus is crisp-tender. Remove the vegetables from the wok.

■ Add *half* of the lamb to the hot wok. Stir-fry for 2 to 3 minutes or to desired doneness. Remove lamb. Repeat with remaining lamb. Return all lamb to the wok. Push lamb from the center of the wok. Stir sauce. Add sauce to the center of the wok. Cook and stir till thickened and bubbly.

■ Return the cooked vegetables to the wok. Stir all ingredients together to coat with sauce. Cover and cook about 1 minute more or till heated through. Stir in nuts and lemon peel. Serve immediately over hot cooked couscous or rice. Makes 4 servings.

Nutrition information per serving: 334 calories, 29 g protein, 23 g carbohydrate, 15 g fat (4 g saturated), 68 mg cholesterol, 464 mg sodium, 660 mg potassium.

Sweet-and-Sour Chicken Livers

SWEET-AND-SOUR CHICKEN LIVERS

½ cup water
3 tablespoons sugar
2 tablespoons vinegar
1 tablespoon cornstarch
1 tablespoon soy sauce
1 tablespoon cooking oil
1 clove garlic, minced
1 teaspoon grated gingerroot
3 medium carrots, thinly sliced
   into carrot flowers (see
   directions, page 64) or
   thinly bias sliced (1½ cups)

7 green onions, bias sliced
   into 1-inch lengths (about
   1⅓ cups)
1 medium sweet red or green
   pepper, cut into ¾-inch
   pieces (¾ cup)
12 ounces chicken livers, halved
3 cups hot cooked rice
   Flowering kale (optional)
   Carrot shreds (optional)

Here are chicken livers like you've never tasted before—stir-fried and coated with a rich sweet-and-sour sauce.

■ For sauce, in a small bowl stir together the water, sugar, vinegar, cornstarch, and soy sauce. Set aside.

■ Pour cooking oil into a wok or large skillet. (Add more oil as necessary during cooking.) Preheat over medium-high heat. Stir-fry garlic and gingerroot in hot oil for 15 seconds. Add carrots; stir-fry for 2½ minutes. Add green onions and red or green pepper; stir-fry about 1½ minutes more or till vegetables are crisp-tender. Remove the vegetables from the wok.

■ Add the chicken livers to the hot wok. Stir-fry for 3 to 4 minutes or till livers are just pink in the center. Push the chicken livers from the center of the wok. Stir sauce. Add the sauce to the center of the wok. Cook and stir till thickened and bubbly.

■ Return the cooked vegetables to the wok. Stir all ingredients together to coat with sauce. Cook and stir about 1 minute more or till heated through. Serve immediately over hot cooked rice. If desired, garnish with flowering kale and carrot shreds. Makes 4 servings.

Nutrition information per serving: 414 calories, 21 g protein, 65 g carbohydrate, 8 g fat (2 g saturated), 402 mg cholesterol, 318 mg sodium, 477 mg potassium.

LEMONGRASS CHICKEN

4 large boneless, skinless chicken breast halves (1 pound total)
3 tablespoons water
3 tablespoons white vinegar
2 tablespoons fish sauce
1 teaspoon sugar
1 teaspoon cornstarch
1 teaspoon grated gingerroot
1 tablespoon finely chopped fresh lemongrass (2 stalks) or ½ teaspoon finely shredded lemon peel
1 tablespoon cooking oil
3 cloves garlic, minced

2 medium onions, thinly sliced and separated into rings (1½ cups)
1 tablespoon seeded fresh red chili peppers cut into thin strips (see tip, page 27) (optional)
½ cup fresh basil leaves
3 cups hot cooked Chinese egg noodles
Lemon twists (see directions for Citrus Twists, page 200) (optional)
Fresh basil leaves (optional)

■ Rinse chicken and pat dry. Cut chicken into ¾-inch pieces. For marinade, in a medium mixing bowl stir together the water, vinegar, fish sauce, sugar, cornstarch, gingerroot, and ⅛ teaspoon *pepper*. Add chicken and lemongrass or lemon peel. Stir to coat. Let stand at room temperature for 30 minutes, stirring occasionally. Drain chicken, reserving marinade.

■ Pour cooking oil into a wok or large skillet. (Add more oil as necessary during cooking.) Preheat over medium-high heat. Stir-fry garlic in hot oil for 15 seconds. Add onions and, if desired, chili peppers. Stir-fry about 3 minutes or till onions are crisp-tender. Remove. Add *half* of the chicken to the hot wok. Stir-fry for 2 to 3 minutes or till no pink remains. Remove from the wok. Repeat with remaining chicken. Return all chicken to the wok. Add reserved marinade.

■ Return vegetables to the wok. Stir all ingredients together to coat with marinade. Cook and stir about 1 minute or till heated through. Add the ½ cup basil leaves; toss to mix. Serve immediately over noodles. If desired, garnish with lemon twists and more basil leaves. Makes 4 servings.

NOTE: If desired, omit the ½ cup fresh basil leaves. Instead, substitute ½ cup fresh torn *spinach leaves*. Also add 1 teaspoon *dried basil* to the marinade.

Nutrition information per serving: 371 calories, 33 g protein, 38 g carbohydrate, 9 g fat (2 g saturated), 109 mg cholesterol, 688 mg sodium, 391 mg potassium.

SESAME CHICKEN AND VEGETABLES

4 dried mushrooms
4 medium boneless, skinless
    chicken breast halves
    (12 ounces total)
1 cup fresh pea pods or ½ of a
    6-ounce package frozen pea
    pods, thawed
½ of an 8-ounce package frozen
    whole baby sweet corn,
    thawed, or one 8¾-ounce
    can whole baby sweet corn,
    drained
⅓ cup chicken broth
2 tablespoons fish sauce

2 teaspoons cornstarch
1 teaspoon sesame oil
½ teaspoon sugar
4 ounces rice sticks or 3 cups
    hot cooked rice
1 tablespoon cooking oil
1 teaspoon grated gingerroot
3 cups thinly sliced bok choy
    or shredded cabbage
1 medium sweet red pepper, cut
    into thin strips (1 cup)
1 tablespoon sesame seed,
    toasted

Make your Oriental dishes as beautiful as they are delicious with simple garnishes. For the photo on the cover, we garnished **Sesame Chicken and Vegetables** *with yellow pepper strips, purple basil leaves, a carrot flower, and green onion curls.*

■ In a mixing bowl soak mushrooms for 30 minutes in enough warm water to cover. Rinse well and squeeze to drain thoroughly. Cut into thin strips, discarding stems. Meanwhile, rinse chicken and pat dry. Cut into thin bite-size strips. Slice pea pods diagonally in half. Cut corn in half crosswise. Set all ingredients aside. For sauce, in a small bowl stir together the chicken broth, fish sauce, cornstarch, sesame oil, and sugar. Set aside. If using rice sticks, in a large saucepan cook rice sticks in boiling water for 1 to 2 minutes or just till tender. Drain and keep warm.

■ Pour cooking oil into a wok or large skillet. (Add more oil as necessary during cooking.) Preheat over medium-high heat. Stir-fry gingerroot in hot oil for 15 seconds. Add bok choy or cabbage; stir-fry for 1½ minutes. Add red pepper, fresh pea pods (if using), and baby corn. Stir-fry about 1½ minutes or till crisp-tender. Remove. Add the chicken to the hot wok. Stir-fry for 2 to 3 minutes or till no pink remains. Push chicken from the center. Stir sauce. Add sauce to the center. Cook and stir till thickened and bubbly.

■ Return the cooked vegetables to the wok. Add mushrooms and, if using, thawed pea pods. Stir all ingredients together to coat with sauce. Cook and stir about 1 minute more or till heated through. Serve immediately over hot cooked rice sticks or rice. Sprinkle with sesame seed. Makes 4 servings.

Nutrition information per serving: 328 calories, 27 g protein, 34 g carbohydrate, 9 g fat
(2 g saturated), 54 mg cholesterol, 734 mg sodium, 536 mg potassium.

CHICKEN STIR-FRY OVER PASTA

A little Chinese, a little Italian, a little American—that's the best way to describe this dish. Tender chicken and crunchy vegetables team up with pasta for a delicious combo.

4 large boneless, skinless chicken breast halves (1 pound total)
½ cup water
3 tablespoons soy sauce
3 tablespoons dry sherry
2 teaspoons cornstarch
½ teaspoon sugar
⅛ teaspoon pepper
1 tablespoon cooking oil
2 cloves garlic, minced

1½ cups thinly sliced cauliflower flowerets
2 medium carrots, cut into julienne strips (1 cup)
2 small zucchini, sliced ¼ inch thick (2 cups)
1 small onion, sliced into thin wedges (⅔ cup)
3 cups hot cooked spaghetti or linguine

■ Rinse chicken and pat dry. Cut into 1-inch pieces. For sauce, in a small bowl stir together the water, soy sauce, dry sherry, cornstarch, sugar, and pepper. Set aside.

■ Pour cooking oil into a wok or 12-inch skillet. (Add more oil as necessary during cooking.) Preheat over medium-high heat. Stir-fry garlic in hot oil for 15 seconds. Add cauliflower; stir-fry for 1 minute. Add carrots; stir-fry for 3 to 4 minutes more or till crisp-tender. Remove the vegetables from the wok. Add the zucchini and onion to the wok. Stir-fry for 3 to 4 minutes or till vegetables are crisp-tender. Remove the vegetables from the wok.

■ Add *half* of the chicken to the hot wok. Stir-fry for 2 to 3 minutes or till no pink remains. Remove the chicken from the wok. Repeat with remaining chicken. Return all the chicken to the wok. Push chicken from the center of the wok. Stir sauce. Add the sauce to the center of the wok. Cook and stir till thickened and bubbly.

■ Return the cooked vegetables to the wok. Stir all ingredients together to coat with sauce. Cook and stir about 1 minute more or till heated through. Serve immediately over hot cooked spaghetti or linguine. Makes 4 servings.

Nutrition information per serving: 394 calories, 34 g protein, 42 g carbohydrate, 8 g fat (2 g saturated), 72 mg cholesterol, 860 mg sodium, 722 mg potassium.

BLACK-BEAN-SAUCED CHICKEN

4 large boneless, skinless
   chicken breast halves
   (1 pound total)
⅓ cup water
1 tablespoon soy sauce
2 teaspoons cornstarch
½ teaspoon sugar
½ teaspoon instant chicken
   bouillon granules
1 tablespoon cooking oil
2 cloves garlic, minced

1 pound fresh asparagus, cut
   into 1-inch pieces (3 cups)
   or one 10-ounce package
   frozen cut asparagus,
   thawed
1 medium onion, cut into thin
   wedges (¾ cup)
1 tablespoon fermented black
   beans, chopped
3 cups hot cooked rice

CHINESE SPECIALTY
In China, black beans are as common as catsup is in the United States. Black beans have a pleasing wine-like flavor that complements meat and poultry, asparagus, and broccoli.

■ Rinse chicken and pat dry. Cut into ¾-inch pieces. For sauce, in a small bowl stir together the water, soy sauce, cornstarch, sugar, and chicken bouillon granules. Set aside.

■ Pour cooking oil into a wok or large skillet. (Add more oil as necessary during cooking.) Preheat over medium-high heat. Stir-fry garlic in hot oil for 15 seconds. If using fresh asparagus, stir-fry for 1 minute. Add thawed asparagus (if using), onion, and black beans; stir-fry about 3 minutes more or till vegetables are crisp-tender. Remove vegetables from the wok.

■ Add *half* of the chicken to the hot wok. Stir-fry for 2 to 3 minutes or till no pink remains. Remove the chicken from the wok. Repeat with remaining chicken. Return all chicken to the wok. Push the chicken from the center of the wok. Stir sauce. Add the sauce to the center of the wok. Cook and stir till thickened and bubbly.

■ Return the cooked vegetables to the wok. Stir all ingredients together to coat with sauce. Cook and stir about 1 minute more or till heated through. Serve immediately over hot cooked rice. Makes 4 servings.

Nutrition information per serving: 420 calories, 35 g protein, 51 g carbohydrate, 8 g fat (2 g saturated), 72 mg cholesterol, 588 mg sodium, 629 mg potassium.

PLUM DELICIOUS CHICKEN STIR-FRY

Crunchy pea pods, tender chicken, and fresh fruit glazed with a sweet-and-sour sauce make this a sensational stir-fry. You can use plums, apricots, or pears for the fruit. For best flavor, choose whichever fruit is in season.

4 medium boneless, skinless chicken breast halves (12 ounces total)
2 cups fresh pea pods **or** one 6-ounce package frozen pea pods, thawed
¼ cup red plum jam **or** currant jelly
3 tablespoons rice vinegar **or** white vinegar
3 tablespoons soy sauce

1 tablespoon cornstarch
1 tablespoon cooking oil
1 small onion, thinly sliced and separated into rings (⅔ cup)
4 plums **or** apricots, pitted and cut into wedges (12 ounces total), **or** 2 cups sliced pears
3 cups hot cooked Chinese egg noodles **or** hot cooked rice
Plum wedges (optional)

■ Rinse chicken and pat dry. Cut into thin bite-size strips. Slice pea pods diagonally in half. For sauce, in a small bowl stir together the jam or jelly, rice vinegar or white vinegar, soy sauce, and cornstarch. Set aside.

■ Pour cooking oil into a wok or 12-inch skillet. (Add more oil as necessary during cooking.) Preheat over medium-high heat. Stir-fry onion in hot oil for 2 minutes. Add fresh pea pods, if using. Stir-fry about 1 minute more or till vegetables are crisp-tender. Remove the vegetables from the wok.

■ Add the chicken to the hot wok. Stir-fry for 2 to 3 minutes or till no pink remains. Push the chicken from center of the wok. Stir sauce. Add the sauce to the center of the wok. Cook and stir till thickened and bubbly.

■ Return the cooked vegetables to the wok. Add plums, apricots, or pears and, if using, thawed pea pods. Stir all ingredients together to coat with sauce. Cook and stir about 1 minute more or till heated through. Serve immediately over hot cooked Chinese egg noodles or rice. If desired, garnish with plum wedges. Makes 4 servings.

Nutrition information per serving: 432 calories, 29 g protein, 61 g carbohydrate, 9 g fat (2 g saturated), 91 mg cholesterol, 835 mg sodium, 486 mg potassium.

Plum Delicious Chicken Stir-Fry

CHICKEN DOMBURI

炒
飯
烹
飪

JAPANESE SPECIALTY

Instead of eating sandwiches for lunch, workers in Japan often have a one-dish meal of rice or noodles with beef, fish, or chicken. These one-dish meals are usually served in a deep pottery or porcelain bowl called a domburi.

6 *dried mushrooms*
4 *large boneless, skinless*
   chicken breast halves
   (1 pound total)
1 *cup water*
¼ *cup mirin or dry sherry*
¼ *cup soy sauce*
1 *tablespoon sugar*
1 *tablespoon cooking oil*

1 *teaspoon grated gingerroot*
2 *medium carrots, chopped*
   (1 cup)
2 *medium onions, chopped*
   (1 cup)
2 *beaten eggs*
3 *cups hot cooked rice*
2 *green onions, slivered (about*
   ⅓ cup) (optional)

■ In a small mixing bowl soak mushrooms for 30 minutes in enough warm water to cover. Rinse well and squeeze to drain thoroughly. Slice thinly, discarding stems. Meanwhile, rinse chicken and pat dry. Cut into thin bite-size strips. For sauce, in a small bowl stir together the water, mirin or dry sherry, soy sauce, and sugar. Set aside.

■ Pour cooking oil into a wok or large skillet. (Add more oil as necessary during cooking.) Preheat over medium-high heat. Stir-fry gingerroot in hot oil for 15 seconds. Add the carrots and onions. Stir-fry for 3 to 4 minutes or till vegetables are crisp-tender. Remove the vegetables from the wok.

■ Add *half* of the chicken to the hot wok. Stir-fry for 2 to 3 minutes or till no pink remains. Remove the chicken from the wok. Repeat with remaining chicken. Return all chicken to the wok.

■ Add the sauce to the wok. Return the cooked vegetables to the wok. Add the mushrooms. Stir all ingredients together to coat with sauce. Bring to boiling; reduce heat. Cover and simmer for 1 minute. Pour the eggs into the wok in a steady stream while stirring 2 or 3 times to create shreds. Serve immediately in individual serving bowls over hot cooked rice. If desired, garnish with slivered onions. Makes 4 servings.

Nutrition information per serving: 500 calories, 36 g protein, 60 g carbohydrate, 10 g fat (2 g saturated), 178 mg cholesterol, 1,144 mg sodium, 618 mg potassium.

GARLIC CHICKEN

4 medium boneless, skinless
   chicken breast halves
   (12 ounces total)
½ cup water
2 tablespoons soy sauce
1 tablespoon cornstarch
1 tablespoon rice wine
   or dry white wine
½ teaspoon instant chicken
   bouillon granules
1 tablespoon cooking oil

10 cloves garlic, minced
   (1 tablespoon)
6 ounces fresh mushrooms,
   sliced (about 2 cups)
1 medium leek, thinly sliced
   (½ cup) or 4 green onions,
   thinly sliced (½ cup)
½ of an 8-ounce can sliced
   water chestnuts, drained
3 cups hot cooked rice

THAI SPECIALTY
Ten cloves of garlic may sound like a lot, but you'll be surprised by the mellow flavor of this dish. For an easy option, try using bottled minced garlic instead of the whole cloves of garlic. Bottled garlic gives great flavor and requires no peeling and mincing.

■ Rinse chicken; pat dry. Cut into ½-inch pieces. For sauce, stir together the water, soy sauce, cornstarch, wine, and chicken bouillon granules. Set aside.

■ Pour cooking oil into a wok or 10-inch skillet. (Add more oil as necessary during cooking.) Preheat over medium-high heat. Stir-fry garlic in hot oil for 15 seconds. Add mushrooms and leek or green onions. Stir-fry about 1 minute or till vegetables are tender. Remove the vegetables from the wok. Add the chicken to the hot wok. Stir-fry for 2 to 3 minutes or till no pink remains. Push the chicken from the center of the wok. Stir sauce. Add the sauce to the center of the wok. Cook and stir till thickened and bubbly.

■ Return the vegetables to the wok. Add water chestnuts. Stir all ingredients together to coat with sauce. Cook and stir about 1 minute more or till heated through. Serve immediately over hot cooked rice. Makes 4 servings.

Nutrition information per serving: 393 calories, 26 g protein, 55 g carbohydrate, 7 g fat (1 g saturated), 54 mg cholesterol, 687 mg sodium, 452 mg potassium.

GARLIC CHICKEN AND SPINACH: Prepare as directed above, *except* use a wok or 12-inch skillet and stir in 3 cups torn *spinach leaves* when adding the water chestnuts.

Nutrition information per serving: 403 calories, 27 g protein, 56 g carbohydrate, 7 g fat (1 g saturated), 54 mg cholesterol, 720 mg sodium, 686 mg potassium.

TANGERINE-PEEL CHICKEN

CHINESE SPECIALTY

Another Szechwan specialty is Tangerine-Peel Beef. Follow the recipe at right, except substitute 1 pound beef top round steak, thinly sliced across the grain, for the chicken.

2 1x½-inch pieces purchased dried tangerine peel, or *Dried Tangerine Peel* (see recipe, page 82), or 1 tablespoon finely shredded fresh tangerine or orange peel
4 large boneless, skinless chicken breast halves (1 pound total)
¼ cup water
2 tablespoons soy sauce
1 tablespoon rice wine or *dry white wine*

1 teaspoon cornstarch
1 teaspoon sugar
½ teaspoon whole Szechwan peppers, crushed, **or** whole black peppers, crushed
1 tablespoon cooking oil
2 cloves garlic, minced
4 dried red chili peppers (see tip, page 27)
12 green onions, cut into 2-inch-long slivers (2 cups)
3 cups hot cooked rice

■ If using dried peel, in a small bowl soak peel for 30 minutes in enough warm water to cover. Drain. Cut the peel into ⅛-inch-wide pieces. Meanwhile, rinse chicken and pat dry. Cut into thin bite-size strips. For sauce, in a small bowl stir together the water, soy sauce, rice wine or dry white wine, cornstarch, sugar, and Szechwan or black peppers. Set aside.

■ Pour cooking oil into a wok or large skillet. (Add more oil as necessary during cooking.) Preheat over medium-high heat. Stir-fry garlic in hot oil for 15 seconds. Add *half* of the chicken and *half* of the chili peppers. Stir-fry for 2 to 3 minutes or till no pink remains in chicken. Remove from the wok. Repeat with remaining chicken and chili peppers. Return all chicken and chili peppers to the wok. Push from the center of the wok. Stir sauce. Add the sauce to the center of the wok. Cook and stir till thickened and bubbly.

■ Add the green onion slivers and the dried or fresh tangerine or orange peel to the wok. Stir all ingredients together to coat with sauce. Cook and stir about 1 minute more or till heated through. Serve immediately over hot cooked rice. Makes 4 servings.

Nutrition information per serving: 426 calories, 33 g protein, 54 g carbohydrate, 8 g fat (2 g saturated), 72 mg cholesterol, 595 mg sodium, 592 mg potassium.

MOO GOO GAI PAN

4 medium boneless, skinless
  chicken breast halves
  (12 ounces total)
½ cup chicken broth
2 tablespoons soy sauce
2 tablespoons rice wine
  or dry white wine
4 teaspoons cornstarch
½ teaspoon sugar
1 tablespoon cooking oil
3 cloves garlic, minced
2 medium carrots, thinly sliced
  into carrot flowers (see
  directions, page 64) or
  thinly bias sliced (1 cup)

8 ounces whole small fresh
  mushrooms (3 cups) or
  large fresh mushrooms,
  halved (3 cups)
2 cups fresh pea pods or one
  6-ounce package frozen pea
  pods, thawed
½ of an 8-ounce can sliced
  water chestnuts, drained
3 cups hot cooked rice

CHINESE SPECIALTY
In Chinese, "moo goo" means mushrooms, "gai" means chicken, and "pan" means slices. Put them all together and you have sliced chicken with mushrooms. We added carrots, pea pods, and water chestnuts to this version for color and crunch.

■ Rinse chicken and pat dry. Cut into thin bite-size strips. For sauce, in a small bowl stir together the chicken broth, soy sauce, rice wine or white wine, cornstarch, and sugar. Set aside.

■ Pour cooking oil into a wok or large skillet. (Add more oil as necessary during cooking.) Preheat over medium-high heat. Stir-fry garlic in hot oil for 15 seconds. Add carrots; stir-fry for 3 minutes. Add mushrooms and, if using, fresh pea pods; stir-fry about 1 minute more or till carrots and pea pods are crisp-tender. Remove the vegetables from the wok.

■ Add the chicken to the hot wok. Stir-fry for 2 to 3 minutes or till no pink remains. Push the chicken from the center of the wok. Stir sauce. Add the sauce to the center of the wok. Cook and stir till thickened and bubbly.

■ Return the cooked vegetables to the wok. Add water chestnuts and, if using, thawed pea pods. Stir all ingredients together to coat with sauce. Cook and stir about 1 minute more or till heated through. Serve immediately over hot cooked rice. Makes 4 servings.

Nutrition information per serving: 439 calories, 29 g protein, 62 g carbohydrate, 7 g fat (1 g saturated), 54 mg cholesterol, 685 mg sodium, 779 mg potassium.

FIVE-SPICE CHICKEN AND SHRIMP

Five-spice powder gives a sweet spiciness to this tasty shrimp and chicken dish.

8 ounces fresh or *frozen shrimp in shells*

3 medium boneless, skinless chicken breast halves (9 ounces total)

2 tablespoons soy sauce

½ teaspoon purchased five-spice powder or *Five-Spice Powder (see recipe, page 82)*

½ cup water

¼ cup dry sherry

4 teaspoons cornstarch

½ teaspoon instant chicken bouillon granules

1 tablespoon cooking oil

1 clove garlic, minced

3 cups broccoli flowerets

1 medium carrot, thinly bias sliced (½ cup)

⅓ cup broken walnuts or *sliced almonds, toasted*

3 cups hot cooked rice

■ Thaw shrimp, if frozen. Peel and devein shrimp. Cut shrimp in half lengthwise. Rinse chicken and pat dry. Cut into ¾-inch pieces. In a small mixing bowl combine chicken, soy sauce, and five-spice powder; let stand at room temperature for 15 minutes. For sauce, in a small bowl stir together the water, dry sherry, cornstarch, and chicken bouillon granules. Set aside.

■ Pour cooking oil into a wok or large skillet. (Add more oil as necessary during cooking.) Preheat over medium-high heat. Stir-fry garlic in hot oil for 15 seconds. Add broccoli and carrot; stir-fry for 3 to 4 minutes or till crisp-tender. Remove the vegetables from the wok.

■ Add the chicken to the hot wok. Stir-fry for 2 to 3 minutes or till no pink remains. Remove the chicken from the wok. Add the shrimp to the hot wok. Stir-fry for 2 to 3 minutes or till shrimp turn pink. Return the chicken to the wok. Push the chicken and the shrimp from the center of the wok. Stir the sauce. Add the sauce to the center of the wok. Cook and stir till thickened and bubbly.

■ Return the cooked vegetables to the hot wok. Stir all ingredients together to coat with sauce. Cook and stir about 1 minute more or till heated through. Stir in the walnuts or almonds. Serve immediately over hot cooked rice. Makes 4 servings.

Nutrition information per serving: 457 calories, 29 g protein, 53 g carbohydrate, 13 g fat (2 g saturated), 94 mg cholesterol, 756 mg sodium, 580 mg potassium.

ORIENTAL TURKEY TORTILLAS

3 turkey breast tenderloin steaks
   (12 ounces total) or 4
   medium boneless, skinless
   chicken breast halves
   (12 ounces total)
½ cup water
2 tablespoons purchased plum
   sauce or Plum Sauce
   (see recipe, page 82)
1 tablespoon soy sauce

2 teaspoons cornstarch
1 tablespoon cooking oil
2 cups loose-pack frozen
   broccoli, carrots, water
   chestnuts, and red peppers,
   thawed and drained
½ cup alfalfa sprouts
8 6-inch flour tortillas, warmed
   (see tip, page 159)

We've taken a Mexican tortilla and packed it with all-American turkey or chicken and Oriental ingredients. The result is a terrific entrée sure to please western or eastern palates.

■ Rinse turkey or chicken and pat dry. Cut into thin bite-size strips. For sauce, stir together the water, plum sauce, soy sauce, and cornstarch. Pour cooking oil into a wok or large skillet. (Add more oil as necessary during cooking.) Preheat over medium-high heat. Stir-fry thawed vegetables about 2 minutes or till crisp-tender. Remove the vegetables from the wok.

■ Add turkey to hot wok. Stir-fry 2 to 3 minutes or till no pink remains. Push turkey from center of wok. Stir sauce. Add sauce to center of wok. Cook and stir till thickened and bubbly. Return vegetables to wok. Stir ingredients together to coat with sauce. Cook and stir about 1 minute more or till heated through. Spoon about ⅓ *cup* turkey mixture and some alfalfa sprouts into the center of a tortilla. Fold tortilla pocket-style (see directions, page 28) or roll up jelly-roll-style. Repeat. Serve immediately. Serves 4.

Nutrition information per serving: 323 calories, 24 g protein, 40 g carbohydrate, 8 g fat (1 g saturated), 54 mg cholesterol, 611 mg sodium, 255 mg potassium.

BROTH OPTIONS

Because making your own beef or chicken broth takes time you may not have, there are several convenience products you may use instead. Choose from ready-to-use canned regular or sodium-reduced broth, condensed broth, and bouillon granules or cubes. Bouillon granules are especially convenient because they allow you to make small amounts (less than a cup) of broth.

Curry Fish

CURRY FISH

1 pound fresh or frozen
   swordfish, shark, sea bass,
   tuna, monkfish, or cusk
   steaks or fillets (1 inch
   thick)
½ cup chicken broth
2 tablespoons fish sauce
1 tablespoon red curry paste
½ teaspoon sugar
1 tablespoon cooking oil

2 medium carrots, cut into
   julienne strips (1 cup)
2 stalks celery, cut into julienne
   strips (1 cup)
1 8-ounce can bamboo shoots,
   drained and cut into
   julienne strips
3 cups hot cooked rice
   Lemon and/or lime wedges
   (optional)
   Cilantro leaves (optional)

■ Thaw fish, if frozen. Cut into 1-inch cubes; discard skin and bones. For sauce, combine broth, fish sauce, curry paste, and sugar. Pour oil into a wok or large skillet. (Add more oil as necessary during cooking.) Preheat over medium-high heat. Add carrots and celery; stir-fry 3 minutes. Add bamboo shoots; stir-fry 1 minute or till crisp-tender. Remove. Add *half* the fish to the hot wok. Stir-fry 3 to 6 minutes or till fish flakes easily, stirring gently. Remove. Repeat with remaining fish. Return all fish; push from center.

■ Stir sauce. Add sauce to the center. Cook and stir till slightly thickened. Return vegetables to wok. Stir ingredients to coat with sauce. Simmer 1 to 2 minutes or till sauce is slightly reduced. Serve immediately with rice. If desired, garnish with lemon and/or lime wedges and cilantro. Serves 4.

Nutrition information per serving: 396 calories, 28 g protein, 50 g carbohydrate, 9 g fat (2 g saturated), 43 mg cholesterol, 843 mg sodium, 650 mg potassium.

FISH AND MEAT FOR STIR-FRYING

What kinds of fish and meat are best for stir-frying? For fish stir-fries, select only firm fish as directed in the recipes. For chicken stir-fries, use boneless, skinless chicken breast halves or thighs. (If you'd like to skin and bone chicken breasts yourself, follow our instructions on page 67.) When a recipe calls for pork, beef, or lamb, choose cuts from the shoulder, loin, sirloin, flank, round, or chuck.

FISH WITH FRESH TOMATOES

VIETNAMESE SPECIALTY

Each country in Southeast Asia has its own version of fish sauce. Vietnam has "nuoc mam," which is used as frequently in Vietnamese cooking as soy sauce is in Chinese cooking.

1¼ pounds fresh or frozen swordfish, shark, sea bass, tuna, monkfish, or cusk steaks or fillets (1 inch thick)
2 tablespoons fish sauce
1 teaspoon sugar
¼ teaspoon pepper

3 large tomatoes or 8 or 9 plum tomatoes, seeded and cut into bite-size pieces (about 3¾ cups)
1 tablespoon cooking oil
6 green onions, bias sliced into 1-inch pieces (1 cup)
2 cloves garlic, minced
3 cups hot cooked vermicelli or rice

■ Thaw fish, if frozen. Cut fish into 1-inch cubes, discarding any skin and bones. In a medium mixing bowl stir together the fish sauce, sugar, and pepper. Stir in tomatoes. Set aside.

■ Pour cooking oil into a wok or large skillet. (Add more oil as necessary during cooking.) Preheat over medium-high heat. Stir-fry green onions and garlic in hot oil about 1½ minutes or till tender. Remove from the wok. Add *half* of the fish to the hot wok. Stir-fry for 3 to 6 minutes or till fish flakes easily, being careful not to break up pieces. Remove from wok. Repeat with remaining fish. Return all of the fish and onion mixture to the wok. Add the tomato mixture. Stir gently to combine. Cover wok and cook for 2 minutes. Serve immediately with vermicelli or rice. Makes 4 servings.

Nutrition information per serving: 385 calories, 35 g protein, 38 g carbohydrate, 11 g fat (2 g saturated), 91 mg cholesterol, 755 mg sodium, 722 mg potassium.

USING NONSTICK SPRAY COATING

To help cut fat calories, use nonstick spray coating in place of some of the cooking oil when stir-frying. Start by spraying the room-temperature wok or skillet and preheating it over medium heat. Then, stir-fry the vegetables. But, to prevent sticking, you'll need to add up to 1 tablespoon of cooking oil before stir-frying the meat. (Spraying a hot surface with nonstick coating is not recommended.)

TERIYAKI FISH STIR-FRY

1 pound fresh or frozen
　　swordfish, shark, sea bass,
　　tuna, monkfish, or cusk
　　steaks or fillets (1 inch
　　thick)
½ cup water
2 tablespoons soy sauce
2 tablespoons rice wine
　　or dry white wine
1 tablespoon cornstarch
1 teaspoon sugar
½ teaspoon dry mustard
⅛ teaspoon pepper

1 tablespoon cooking oil
1 teaspoon grated gingerroot
1 clove garlic, minced
1 pound fresh asparagus, bias
　　sliced into 1-inch lengths,
　　or one 10-ounce package
　　frozen cut asparagus,
　　thawed
1 large sweet red pepper,
　　cut into 1-inch pieces
　　(1⅓ cups)
3 cups hot cooked rice
　　Sliced almonds (optional)

Teriyaki originally referred to a sweet soy-based glaze used in Japanese cooking. Now it has come to mean anything that shares this sweetened soy sauce flavor.

■ Thaw fish, if frozen. Cut fish into 1-inch cubes, discarding any skin and bones. For sauce, in a small bowl stir together the water, soy sauce, rice wine or dry white wine, cornstarch, sugar, dry mustard, and pepper. Set aside.

■ Pour cooking oil into a wok or large skillet. (Add more oil as necessary during cooking.) Preheat over medium-high heat. Stir-fry gingerroot and garlic in hot oil for 15 seconds. Add fresh asparagus, if using; stir-fry for 2 minutes. Or, add frozen asparagus, if using; stir-fry for 1 minute. Add red pepper; stir-fry about 2 minutes more or till vegetables are crisp-tender. Remove the vegetables from the wok.

■ Add *half* of the fish to the hot wok. Stir-fry for 3 to 6 minutes or till fish flakes easily, being careful not to break up pieces. Gently remove the fish from the wok. Repeat with remaining fish. Return all fish to the wok. Push fish from the center of the wok. Stir sauce. Add the sauce to the center of the wok. Cook and stir till thickened and bubbly.

■ Return the cooked vegetables to the wok. Stir all ingredients together to coat with sauce. Cook and stir gently about 1 minute more or till heated through. Serve immediately over hot cooked rice. If desired, garnish with sliced almonds. Makes 4 servings.

Nutrition information per serving: 409 calories, 30 g protein, 52 g carbohydrate, 9 g fat (2 g saturated), 43 mg cholesterol, 618 mg sodium, 786 mg potassium.

SQUID WITH VEGETABLES

To remove the head and tentacles from the squid, hold the squid's body in one hand and firmly grasp the tentacles with the other hand. Then, pull the tentacles and head out of the body. Remove and discard the head; reserve the tentacles.

½ cup dried wood ears
1½ pounds fresh **or** frozen squid
    (¾ pound cleaned)
⅓ cup water
2 tablespoons soy sauce
1 teaspoon sugar
1 teaspoon cornstarch
¼ teaspoon instant chicken
    bouillon granules
1 tablespoon cooking oil
½ teaspoon sesame oil

1 to 2 teaspoons grated
    gingerroot
1 clove garlic, minced
3 medium carrots, thinly bias
    sliced (1½ cups)
2 cups fresh pea pods **or** one
    6-ounce package frozen pea
    pods, thawed
3 green onions, sliced (⅓ cup)
3 cups hot cooked rice
    Onion Brush (see directions,
    page 198)(optional)

■ Soak wood ears 30 minutes in enough warm water to cover. Rinse well; squeeze to drain. Slice thinly; discard stems. Thaw squid, if frozen. To clean, pull head and tentacles out of body. Cut head off tentacles. Reserve tentacles; discard head. Remove and discard any entrails that remain in the body. Pull out and discard the clear cartilage "pen" running down the back of body. With your fingers, peel skin off outside of body. Rinse body and tentacles; pat dry. Cut squid bodies into 1-inch squares. Set aside.

■ For sauce, in a small bowl stir together the water, soy sauce, sugar, cornstarch, and chicken bouillon granules. Set aside. Pour cooking oil and sesame oil into a wok or large skillet. (Add more cooking oil as necessary during cooking.) Preheat over medium-high heat. Stir-fry gingerroot and garlic in hot oil for 15 seconds. Add carrots and stir-fry for 3 minutes. Add wood ears, fresh pea pods (if using), and green onions. Stir-fry for 2 minutes more or till crisp-tender. Remove the vegetables from the wok.

■ Add the squid pieces and tentacles to the wok. Stir-fry about 2 minutes or till squid is tender. Push from the center of the wok. Stir sauce. Add the sauce to the center of the wok. Cook and stir till thickened and bubbly. Return the cooked vegetables to the wok. Add thawed pea pods, if using. Stir all ingredients together to coat with sauce. Cook and stir about 1 minute more or till heated through. Serve immediately with hot cooked rice. If desired, garnish with an Onion Brush. Makes 4 servings.

Nutrition information per serving: 382 calories, 21 g protein, 61 g carbohydrate, 6 g fat (1 g saturated), 198 mg cholesterol, 635 mg sodium, 667 mg potassium.

SPICY SHRIMP WITH BASIL

1¼ pounds fresh or frozen peeled
       and deveined medium
       shrimp
  2 tablespoons fish sauce
  2 to 3 teaspoons red curry paste
  ½ teaspoon sugar
  1 tablespoon cooking oil

  1 clove garlic, minced
  6 green onions, bias sliced into
       1-inch lengths (1 cup)
  1 cup fresh basil leaves, torn
  3 cups hot cooked rice
       Chili Flower (see directions,
       page 199)(optional)

To offset the fiery hotness of this dish, serve it with stir-fried vegetables or steamed buns.

■ Thaw shrimp, if frozen. Rinse shrimp. Halve shrimp lengthwise; pat dry with paper towels. For sauce, in a small bowl stir together the fish sauce, red curry paste, and sugar. Set aside.

■ Pour cooking oil into a wok or large skillet. (Add more oil as necessary during cooking.) Preheat over medium-high heat. Stir-fry garlic in hot oil for 15 seconds. Add green onions; stir-fry about 1 minute or till tender. Remove. Add *half* of the shrimp to the hot wok. Stir-fry for 2 to 3 minutes or till shrimp turn pink. Remove. Repeat with remaining shrimp. Return all shrimp to the wok. Push shrimp from the center of the wok. Stir sauce. Add the sauce to the center of the wok. Cook and stir till slightly thickened.

■ Return onion mixture to the wok; add basil leaves. Stir all ingredients to coat with sauce. Cover and cook for 1 minute. Serve immediately with hot cooked rice. If desired, garnish with a Chili Flower. Makes 4 servings.

Nutrition information per serving: 353 calories, 29 g protein, 47 g carbohydrate, 5 g fat (1 g saturated), 208 mg cholesterol, 868 mg sodium, 433 mg potassium.

PLAN-AHEAD STIR-FRY

Here's how you can have your stir-fried meal on the table in minutes. Up to 24 hours before mealtime, prepare meat, vegetables, and sauce ingredients as directed in the recipe. Refrigerate ingredients in separate, covered containers until needed. At mealtime, everything will be ready for you to start cooking.

To save preparation time, buy precut fresh vegetables from your supermarket's produce department or salad bar.

SCALLOPS WITH OYSTER SAUCE

You may substitute sea scallops for the bay scallops in this dish, if you wish. To ensure even cooking when using the larger sea scallops, cut them into 1-inch pieces before stir-frying.

1 *pound fresh* or *frozen bay scallops*
⅔ *cup water*
3 *tablespoons oyster sauce*
2 *tablespoons dry sherry*
1 *tablespoon cornstarch*
1 *tablespoon soy sauce*
1 *teaspoon sugar*
1 *tablespoon cooking oil*
1 *medium onion, cut into thin wedges (¾ cup)*

1 *medium green pepper, cut into 1-inch pieces (1 cup)*
1 *medium sweet red pepper, cut into 1-inch pieces (1 cup)*
4 *ounces fresh mushrooms, thinly sliced (1½ cups)*
3 *cups hot cooked rice*
Lemon fan (see directions for Fruit and Vegetable Fans, page 201) (optional)
Fresh rosemary sprig (optional)

■ Thaw scallops, if frozen. Drain scallops well; pat dry with paper towels. For sauce, in a small bowl stir together the water, oyster sauce, dry sherry, cornstarch, soy sauce, and sugar. Set aside.

■ Pour cooking oil into a wok or large skillet. (Add more oil as necessary during cooking.) Preheat over medium-high heat. Add onion; stir-fry for 1 minute. Add green and red peppers; stir-fry for 1 minute. Add mushrooms; stir-fry about 1 minute more or till vegetables are crisp-tender. Remove the vegetables from the wok.

■ Add *half* of the scallops to the hot wok. Stir-fry scallops about 2 minutes or till opaque. Remove the scallops from the wok. Repeat with remaining scallops. Return all scallops to the wok. Push scallops from the center of the wok. Stir sauce. Add the sauce to the center of the wok. Cook and stir till thickened and bubbly.

■ Return the cooked vegetables to the wok. Stir all ingredients together to coat with sauce. Cook and stir about 1 minute more or till heated through. Serve immediately over hot cooked rice. If desired, garnish with a lemon fan and rosemary sprig. Makes 4 servings.

Nutrition information per serving: 383 calories, 25 g protein, 58 g carbohydrate, 5 g fat (1 g saturated), 37 mg cholesterol, 1,067 mg sodium, 647 mg potassium.

Scallops with Oyster Sauce

PHOENIX AND DRAGON

CHINESE SPECIALTY

*In Chinese mythology, the phoenix is a bird that symbolizes feminine beauty and the dragon is a symbol of male virility. When Cantonese chefs combine chicken, considered feminine, with ham or shrimp, regarded as masculine, they usually call the dish some variation of the name **Phoenix and Dragon**. (Pictured on pages 12 and 13.)*

8 ounces fresh or frozen peeled and deveined medium shrimp
2 teaspoons cornstarch
¼ teaspoon ground red pepper
2 medium boneless, skinless chicken breast halves (6 ounces total)
½ cup water
2 tablespoons soy sauce
2 tablespoons dry sherry
1 tablespoon oyster sauce
2 teaspoons cornstarch

½ teaspoon instant chicken bouillon granules
1 tablespoon cooking oil
2 cloves garlic, minced
1 cup thinly sliced carrot half moons (see directions, page 62)
1 cup broccoli flowerets
½ of an 8-ounce can sliced bamboo shoots, drained (½ cup)
1 teaspoon sesame seed, toasted (optional)
3 cups hot cooked rice

■ Thaw shrimp, if frozen. Rinse shrimp. Halve the shrimp lengthwise; pat dry with paper towels. Combine 2 teaspoons cornstarch and red pepper; toss with shrimp. Set aside. Rinse the chicken and pat dry. Cut into ¾-inch pieces; set aside. For sauce, in a small bowl stir together the water, soy sauce, dry sherry, oyster sauce, 2 teaspoons cornstarch, and chicken bouillon granules. Set aside.

■ Pour cooking oil into a wok or large skillet. (Add more oil as necessary during cooking.) Preheat over medium-high heat. Stir-fry garlic in hot oil for 15 seconds. Add carrot and broccoli; stir-fry for 3 to 4 minutes or till vegetables are crisp-tender. Remove the vegetables from the wok. Add the chicken to the hot wok. Stir-fry for 2 to 3 minutes or till no pink remains. Remove the chicken from the wok. Add shrimp and stir-fry for 2 to 3 minutes or till shrimp turn pink. Return chicken to the wok. Push the chicken and shrimp from center of the wok. Stir sauce. Add the sauce to the center of the wok. Cook and stir till thickened and bubbly.

■ Return the cooked vegetables to the wok. Add the bamboo shoots. Stir all ingredients together to coat with sauce. Cook and stir about 1 minute more or till heated through. If desired, sprinkle with toasted sesame seed. Serve immediately over hot cooked rice. Makes 4 servings.

Nutrition information per serving: 378 calories, 25 g protein, 53 g carbohydrate, 6 g fat (1 g saturated), 110 mg cholesterol, 996 mg sodium, 421 mg potassium.

EMERALD-SAUCED SHRIMP

1 pound fresh or frozen peeled
   and deveined medium
   shrimp
2 cups fresh pea pods or
   one 6-ounce package frozen
   pea pods, thawed
⅔ cup chicken broth
2 tablespoons dry sherry
1 tablespoon cornstarch
1 tablespoon soy sauce
1 teaspoon sesame oil

1 tablespoon cooking oil
1 clove garlic, minced
4 green onions, bias sliced into
   1-inch pieces (¾ cup)
6 cups torn spinach
½ of an 8-ounce can sliced
   water chestnuts, drained
   (½ cup)
3 cups warmed chow mein
   noodles

Emerald-Sauced Shrimp gets its name from all the green ingredients—pea pods, green onions, and spinach—that are included in the dish.

■ Thaw shrimp, if frozen. Rinse shrimp. Halve shrimp lengthwise; pat dry with paper towels. Cut the pea pods diagonally in half. For sauce, in a small bowl stir together the chicken broth, dry sherry, cornstarch, soy sauce, and sesame oil. Set aside.

■ Pour cooking oil into a wok or large skillet. (Add more oil as necessary during cooking.) Preheat over medium-high heat. Stir-fry garlic in hot oil for 15 seconds. Add the green onions and, if using, fresh pea pods; stir-fry for 1 minute. Add the spinach; stir-fry about 1 minute more or till spinach is just wilted. Remove the vegetables from the wok.

■ Add *half* of the shrimp to the hot wok. Stir-fry for 2 to 3 minutes or till shrimp turn pink. Remove the shrimp from the wok. Repeat with remaining shrimp. Return all of the shrimp to the wok. Push shrimp from the center of the wok. Stir sauce. Add the sauce to the center of the wok. Cook and stir till thickened and bubbly.

■ Return the cooked vegetables to the wok. Add the thawed pea pods (if using) and the water chestnuts. Stir all ingredients together to coat with sauce. Cook and stir about 1 minute more or till heated through. Serve immediately over warmed chow mein noodles. Makes 4 servings.

Nutrition information per serving: 389 calories, 28 g protein, 34 g carbohydrate, 17 g fat (2 g saturated), 166 mg cholesterol, 800 mg sodium, 932 mg potassium.

ORIENTAL-STYLE MIXED VEGETABLES

Delicate seasoning and a delightful crisp-tender texture make these stir-fried vegetables a wonderful addition to any meal.

1 ounce bean threads
1½ cups fresh green beans, bias sliced into 1-inch pieces, **or** one 9-ounce package frozen cut green beans, thawed
1 tablespoon soy sauce
1 teaspoon sugar
1 teaspoon sesame oil
1 tablespoon cooking oil
1 clove garlic, minced

1 medium onion, cut into thin wedges (¾ cup)
½ cup thinly sliced celery
1 medium sweet red **or** green pepper, cut into thin strips (1 cup)
½ cup sliced fresh mushrooms
½ of an 8-ounce can sliced water chestnuts, drained (½ cup)

■ In a mixing bowl soak the bean threads for 15 minutes in enough warm water to cover. Drain well. Cut into 2- to 3-inch lengths. If using fresh green beans, cook, covered, in a small amount of boiling water for 3½ minutes; drain. For sauce, in a small bowl stir together the soy sauce, sugar, and sesame oil. Set aside.

■ Pour the cooking oil into a wok or large skillet. (Add more oil as necessary during cooking.) Preheat over medium-high heat. Stir-fry garlic in hot oil for 15 seconds. Add the onion and celery; stir-fry for 1½ minutes. Add the red or green pepper and mushrooms; stir-fry about 1½ minutes more or till vegetables are crisp-tender. Remove the vegetables from the wok. Add fresh green beans, if using, to the wok; stir-fry about 3 minutes or till beans are crisp-tender. Or, add thawed green beans, if using; stir-fry for 1½ to 2 minutes or till crisp-tender.

■ Return all of the cooked vegetables to the wok. Add the water chestnuts, bean threads, and sauce. Stir ingredients together to coat with sauce. Cook and stir about 1 minute more or till heated through. Serve immediately. Makes 4 side-dish servings.

Nutrition information per serving: 114 calories, 4 g protein, 16 g carbohydrate, 5 g fat (1 g saturated), 0 mg cholesterol, 276 mg sodium, 346 mg potassium.

SWEET-AND-SOUR VEGETABLES

⅓ cup unsweetened pineapple
    juice
2 tablespoons brown sugar
2 tablespoons white vinegar
2 teaspoons cornstarch
1 tablespoon cooking oil
4 medium carrots, thinly bias
    sliced (2 cups)

1½ cups thinly sliced cauliflower
    flowerets
1 small onion, thinly sliced
    and separated into rings
    (about ½ cup)
1 tablespoon snipped parsley
    or cilantro
¼ cup peanuts, chopped
    (optional)

The contrast of the sweet sugar and the tangy vinegar in the sauce complements the natural flavors of these vegetables.

■ For sauce, in a small mixing bowl stir together the pineapple juice, brown sugar, white vinegar, and cornstarch. Set aside.

■ Pour the cooking oil into a wok or large skillet. (Add more oil as necessary during cooking.) Preheat over medium-high heat. Add the carrots and cauliflower; stir-fry for 2 minutes. Add the onion; stir-fry for 2 to 3 minutes more or till vegetables are crisp-tender. Push vegetables from the center of the wok.

■ Stir sauce. Add the sauce to the center of the wok. Cook and stir till thickened and bubbly. Stir all ingredients together to coat with sauce. Cook and stir about 1 minute more or till heated through. Sprinkle with parsley or cilantro. If desired, top with chopped peanuts. Serve immediately. Makes 4 side-dish servings.

Nutrition information per serving: 119 calories, 2 g protein, 22 g carbohydrate, 4 g fat (0 g saturated), 0 mg cholesterol, 35 mg sodium, 462 mg potassium.

Stir-Fried Baby Corn

STIR-FRIED BABY CORN

½ of an 8-ounce package frozen whole baby sweet corn, thawed, or one 8¾-ounce can whole baby sweet corn, drained
⅓ cup water
1 tablespoon fish sauce
2 teaspoons cornstarch
1 teaspoon sugar
1 tablespoon cooking oil

1 clove garlic, minced
1 teaspoon finely shredded gingerroot
1 medium sweet red or green pepper, cut into julienne strips (1 cup)
1 cup sliced fresh mushrooms Fluted Mushrooms (see directions, page 196) (optional)

Although corn has been used in Oriental dishes for centuries, baby corn is a relative newcomer. Some Oriental cuisines, including those of China, Thailand, and Vietnam, have adopted the ingredient over the past few decades.

■ Cut baby corn into 1-inch pieces. For sauce, in a small bowl stir together the water, fish sauce, cornstarch, and sugar. Set aside.

■ Pour cooking oil into a wok or large skillet. (Add more oil as necessary during cooking.) Preheat over medium-high heat. Stir-fry the garlic and gingerroot in hot oil for 15 seconds. Add the corn, red or green pepper, and mushrooms. Stir-fry for 2 to 3 minutes or till peppers are crisp-tender. Push the vegetables from the center of the wok.

■ Stir sauce. Add the sauce to the center of the wok. Cook and stir till thickened and bubbly. Stir all ingredients together to coat with sauce. Cook and stir about 1 minute more or till heated through. Serve immediately. If desired, garnish with Fluted Mushrooms. Makes 4 side-dish servings.

Nutrition information per serving: 60 calories, 2 g protein, 6 g carbohydrate, 4 g fat (0 g saturated), 0 mg cholesterol, 311 mg sodium, 118 mg potassium.

STIR-FRYING VEGETABLES

Create your own stir-fried side-dish masterpieces from what you have on hand—just as Oriental cooks do. Here are a few tips and a handy stir-fry timing chart to help you along the way. (See "The Stir-Frying Workshop," page 14.)

■ When selecting the vegetables to include in your stir-fry, be sure to select ingredients that will give you a harmonious blend of color, taste, and texture. The possibilities for mixing and matching ingredients are almost limitless.

■ Once you have chosen your ingredients, decide how you will prepare them. You may slice, bias-slice, cut into julienne strips, or roll-cut the vegetables (see directions, pages 62–65). Because the size and shape of the food will affect the stir-frying time, we have included chart entries for vegetables cut different ways.

Ingredients	Quantity	Preparation Directions	Stir-Fry Time
Asparagus (fresh)	12 ounces	Remove tough portion of stem; bias-slice into 1-inch lengths (2¼ cups).	4 to 5 minutes
Asparagus (frozen)	One 10-ounce package frozen cut asparagus	Thaw.	3 minutes
Bean Sprouts (fresh)	4 ounces	Remove roots and rinse off hulls, if present.	1 to 2 minutes
Bok Choy	Half of a small bunch	Thinly slice (2½ cups).	3 minutes
Broccoli (fresh)	8 ounces	Cut flowerets into bite-size pieces; thinly slice stems crosswise (2 cups).	3 to 4 minutes
Broccoli (frozen)	One 10-ounce package frozen cut broccoli	Thaw.	2 to 3 minutes
Cabbage	Half of a small head	Core and shred or chop (3 cups).	3 minutes
Cabbage, Chinese	Half of a small head	Core and shred or chop (3 cups).	1 minute
Carrots	3 medium	Thinly bias-slice (1½ cups).	4 to 5 minutes
	3 medium	Roll-cut (2 cups). Precook, covered, in a small amount of boiling salted water for 3½ minutes; drain.	1 to 2 minutes
	4 medium	Cut into julienne strips (2 cups).	4 minutes
Cauliflower	Half of a medium head	Remove leaves and stem; slice (2¼ cups).	4 minutes
Celery	3 stalks	Thinly bias-slice (1½ cups).	3 minutes
Corn, Baby Sweet (frozen)	One 8-ounce package frozen whole baby sweet corn	Thaw.	2 to 3 minutes

Ingredients	Quantity	Preparation Directions	Stir-Fry Time
Daikon	4 ounces	Peel and cut into julienne strips (1 cup).	3 minutes
Green Beans (fresh)	8 ounces	Bias-slice into 1-inch pieces (1½ cups). Precook, covered, in a small amount of boiling salted water for 4 minutes; drain.	3 minutes
Green Beans (frozen)	One 9-ounce package frozen French-style green beans	Thaw.	1½ minutes
Green Onions	4	Bias-slice into 1-inch lengths (¾ cup).	1½ minutes
Green, Sweet Red, *or* Yellow Pepper	1 medium	Cut into ¾-inch pieces (1 cup).	1½ minutes
Leeks	2	Cut into slivers (1 cup).	1½ minutes
Mushrooms	4 ounces	Slice (1½ cups).	1 minute
Onion	1 medium	Chop (½ cup).	2 minutes
	1 medium	Slice into thin wedges, or slice and separate into rings (¾ cup).	3 minutes
Pea Pods (fresh)	6 to 8 ounces	Remove tips and strings (3 cups).	1 to 2 minutes
Pea Pods (frozen)	One 6-ounce package frozen pea pods	Thaw.	1 to 2 minutes
Snap Peas (fresh)	8 ounces	Remove tips and strings (2 cups).	4 to 5 minutes
Snap Peas (frozen)	One 8-ounce package frozen snap peas	Thaw.	2 minutes
Zucchini *or* Yellow Summer Squash	1 medium	Slice ¼ inch thick (1¼ cups).	3½ minutes

Next, consider the quantity of vegetables you have chosen. You need at least ¾ cup uncooked vegetable for each serving. Limit the amount you stir-fry at one time to about 3 cups.

■ *Now you are ready to start stir-frying. The total cooking time for the dish will be the same as the stir-fry time of the longest-cooking vegetable. Start with the vegetable that will take the most time to stir-fry. Then, add other vegetables at the appropriate times, so they are cooked their recommended amount of stir-fry time. Stir-fry until vegetables are crisp-tender.*

■ *The natural flavors of stir-fried vegetables are enhanced by both Oriental and non-Oriental seasonings and herbs. Try a single seasoning or a combination. If you like, season with soy sauce, lemon juice, salt, pepper, garlic salt, butter, sesame seed, nuts, or any herb that strikes your fancy. For other flavoring suggestions, see Sauces on pages 202–203.*

VEGETABLE CUTTING TECHNIQUES

CUTTING TOMATO WEDGES

Use a cleaver or serrated knife to cut a tomato lengthwise in half. Then remove about ½ inch of the core from each half. Place the halves, cut sides down, on a cutting board and slice lengthwise into wedges. From a medium tomato, cut 6 to 8 pieces for thick wedges or 10 to 12 pieces for thin wedges.

ROLL CUTTING

Roll-cut vegetables by holding a cleaver or chef's knife at a 45-degree angle to the vegetable. Make the first cut, then give the vegetable a quarter- to half-turn and angle-cut again.

Depending on the size, stir-fry timings for roll-cut vegetables can vary from timings for sliced vegetables. Generally, roll-cut vegetables need more cooking time. Some may even require precooking in a small amount of boiling water.

SLICING AND CUTTING HALF MOONS

To slice vegetables, hold a cleaver or chef's knife perpendicular to the vegetable and make the first cut. Make each succeeding cut in the same manner. Thin slices should be no more than ⅛ to ¼ inch thick.

Cut half moons by slicing the vegetable lengthwise in half. Then, slice each vegetable half as described above, making half-circle shapes.

GRATING
Hold unpeeled gingerroot or other vegetable at a 45-degree angle to a fine grater. Move the gingerroot back and forth across the grating surface, making tiny particles, as shown. Wrap any unused gingerroot in a paper towel and store in the refrigerator.

CUTTING JULIENNE STRIPS AND SLIVERS
To cut vegetables into julienne strips, use a cleaver or chef's knife to slice the food into pieces about 2 inches long and about ¼ inch thick.

Then stack the slices and cut them lengthwise again into strips about ⅛ to ¼ inch thick, as shown.

To sliver green onion, garlic, or gingerroot, use a cleaver or chef's knife to cut the food into 2-inch or shorter lengths. Halve each section lengthwise or cut lengthwise into thin slices about ⅛ inch thick. Then, cut each half or slice lengthwise into thin slivers about ⅛ inch thick, as shown.

SHREDDING CABBAGE OR LETTUCE
To shred a head of cabbage or iceberg lettuce by hand, first cut the head through the core into quarters. Then place a quarter section, with a cut side down, on a cutting board. Hold a cleaver or chef's knife perpendicular to the cabbage or lettuce. Slice it into long ⅛- to ¼-inch-thick shreds, as shown.

Shredding done in a blender or on a shredding surface produces much finer pieces. Shredding vegetables by hand is best for stir-frying because it results in larger pieces.

BIAS SLICING

Hold a small chef's knife or cleaver at a 45-degree angle to the vegetable. Make the first cut. Continue making cuts at the same angle as the first cut, spacing the cuts evenly, as shown. Thin bias slices should be no more than ⅛ to ¼ inch thick.

MAKING BROCCOLI AND CAULIFLOWER FLOWERETS

For flowerets, rinse the broccoli or cauliflower under cold running water. Use a paring knife to remove any green leaves. For the broccoli, cut the flowerets from the stalk. Halve any large pieces. For the cauliflower, cut off any brown spots, then cut or break the head into small pieces, as shown.

CUTTING CARROT FLOWERS

Make hand-cut flowers by cutting a large, well-rounded, peeled carrot into 2- to 3-inch lengths. For the petals, make a ¼-inch-deep lengthwise cut with a paring knife. Cut again at an angle to the first cut to form a V-shape wedge; remove wedge. Cut 4 or 5 more wedges, spacing them equally around the carrot. Then slice the carrot ⅛ to ¼ inch thick to form petal-shaped slices, as shown.

Or, for cutout flowers, slice carrot, turnip, parsnip, winter squash, daikon, or zucchini ⅛ to ¼ inch thick. Using a small flower-shape cutter, cut the slice into a flower. If desired, use the vegetable trimmings in soups.

HOW TO USE A CLEAVER

Traditional Chinese cooks consider the cleaver an essential tool in their kitchens. They use it to chop or slice foods, scoop foods from a cutting board into a wok, and to remove scraps from a cutting board.

The three basic types of cleavers are a heavyweight chopper for chopping meats and cutting poultry bones, a lightweight chopper for slicing and cutting soft foods, and a medium-weight chopper that serves both purposes.

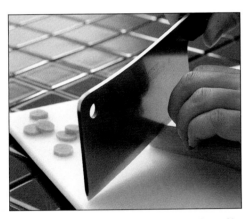

To use a cleaver, grasp the handle with one hand. With your other hand, hold the food with your fingertips curled under and your knuckles against the blade, as shown. Then cut carefully, holding the blade against your knuckles as a guide.

For safety, lift the cleaver just slightly as you cut. With practice, cutting with a cleaver becomes a very smooth and efficient cutting technique.

To chop food, first slice it, then move the cleaver in a seesaw motion, as shown, till the food is chopped.

Care for your cleaver by washing it with hot soapy water after each use. Dry it thoroughly, then apply a thin coat of vegetable oil on both sides of the blade.

For easier slicing, make it a habit to sharpen your cleaver before each use. Use a hand-held sharpening steel or stone for best results. With the steel or stone in one hand, hold the cleaver in the other hand at a 20-degree angle to the sharpener. Draw the blade edge over the sharpener, using a motion that goes across and down at the same time. Turn the blade over, reverse directions, and sharpen the other side the same number of times.

CUTTING MEAT, POULTRY, OR FISH

THINLY BIAS SLICING MEAT

Most cuts of meat are thinly bias-sliced before stir-frying. This ensures maximum tenderness.

To bias-slice meat with ease, first partially freeze fresh meat or partially thaw frozen meat. Allow about 45 to 60 minutes to partially freeze a 1-inch-thick piece of meat. For other thicknesses of meat, adjust the freezing time proportionately. You want the meat to be firm, but not too hard to cut.

Then hold a cleaver or chef's knife at a 45-degree angle to the meat and thinly slice it across the grain, as shown. If necessary, make bite-size pieces by cutting the slices crosswise.

SHREDDING MEAT

First, bias-slice the meat as directed at left. Then, stack a few slices of meat together and cut the slices lengthwise into matchstick-size shreds, as shown.

CUBING MEAT, POULTRY, AND FISH

Trim separable fat and remove bone from meat. Remove any skin, bones, and tendons from chicken. Skin and remove bones from fish. Cut the meat, poultry, or fish lengthwise into 1-inch-wide strips. Then, cut the strips crosswise into cubes, as shown.

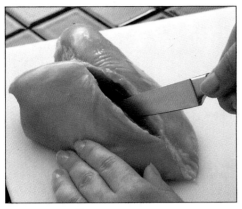

BONING CHICKEN

1. Place the whole chicken breast on a cutting board, skin side up. Starting on one side of the breast, use your hands to pull the skin away from the meat. Discard the skin. Use a thin sharp knife (boning knife) to cut the meat away from one side of the breastbone, as shown. Carefully cut as close to the bone as possible.

CLEANING SHRIMP

1. Devein the shrimp by peeling the shell from it. Use a paring knife to make a shallow slit along the back from the head end to the tail end. Look for the black sand vein that runs along the center of the back. If the vein is there, use the tip of the knife to carefully remove and discard it, as shown. Rinse the shrimp under cold running water.

2. Use a sawing motion to continue cutting the meat away from the rib bones, pressing a flat side of the knife against the bones, as shown. Gently pull the meat away from the bones as you cut.

2. If desired, halve deveined shrimp by placing the shrimp, front side down, on a cutting board. Cut all the way through the shrimp lengthwise, making two pieces, as shown.

Rice and Noodles

Rice and noodles are mainstays of Oriental cuisine—each can be a main ingredient or a base for a stir-fry. In this chapter, we offer a sampling of rice and noodle recipes ranging from the customary, such as Noodle Cakes and Basic Rice, to specialties, such as Thai Fried Rice and Pork and Crab Chow Mein.

Szechwan Chicken-Pasta Salad
(see recipe, page 83)

CHICKEN FRIED RICE

4 medium boneless, skinless
   chicken breast halves
   (12 ounces total)
2 tablespoons soy sauce
⅛ teaspoon pepper
1 tablespoon cooking oil
3 beaten eggs
1 tablespoon cooking oil

2 cloves garlic, minced
8 green onions, diagonally
   sliced into 1-inch pieces
   (1½ cups)
1 cup sliced fresh mushrooms
   or enoki mushrooms
3 cups chilled cooked rice
½ cup frozen peas, thawed

■ Rinse chicken and pat dry. Finely chop the chicken. In a small bowl stir together the soy sauce and pepper. Set aside.

■ Pour 1 tablespoon cooking oil into a wok or large skillet. Preheat over medium heat. Add eggs. Lift and tilt the wok to form a thin sheet of egg. Cook, without stirring, about 2 minutes or just till set. Slide the egg sheet onto a cutting board. Use a knife to finely shred the cooked egg. Set aside.

■ Pour 1 tablespoon cooking oil into the wok or skillet. (Add more oil as necessary during cooking.) Preheat over medium-high heat. Stir-fry garlic in the hot oil for 15 seconds. Add the green onions and, if using, the sliced fresh mushrooms; stir-fry about 1½ minutes or till crisp-tender. Remove vegetables from the wok. Add the chicken to the wok. Stir-fry for 2 to 3 minutes or till no pink remains. Remove chicken from the wok.

■ Add the cooked rice to the wok. Stir-fry for 2 to 3 minutes or till lightly browned. Drizzle the soy sauce mixture over the rice. Return the cooked vegetables and chicken to the wok. Add the shredded egg and thawed peas. Cook and stir till well mixed and heated through. Carefully stir in enoki mushrooms, if using. Serve immediately. Makes 4 servings.

Nutrition information per serving: 467 calories, 31 g protein, 52 g carbohydrate, 14 g fat (3 g saturated), 214 mg cholesterol, 637 mg sodium, 500 mg potassium.

THAI FRIED RICE

12 ounces lean boneless pork
    or *beef*
1 tablespoon cooking oil
2 beaten eggs
1 tablespoon cooking oil
1 medium onion, chopped
    (½ cup)
1 small green **or** *sweet red*
    pepper, chopped (½ cup)

2 to 3 teaspoons chili paste
3 cups chilled cooked rice
2 tablespoons fish sauce
2 tablespoons snipped cilantro
    or *parsley*
    Lime wedges

■ Trim fat from pork or beef. Partially freeze pork or beef. Thinly slice meat across the grain into bite-size strips. Set aside.

■ Pour 1 tablespoon cooking oil into a wok or large skillet. Preheat over medium heat. Add the eggs. Lift and tilt the wok to form a thin sheet of egg. Cook, without stirring, about 2 minutes or just till set. Slide the egg sheet onto a cutting board. Cut into ¾-inch-wide strips. Set aside.

■ Pour 1 tablespoon cooking oil into the wok or skillet. (Add more oil as necessary during cooking.) Preheat over medium-high heat. Add the onion and green pepper; stir-fry for 1½ to 2 minutes or till crisp-tender. Remove the vegetables from the wok. Add the pork or beef to the hot wok. Stir-fry for 2 to 3 minutes or till no pink remains.

■ Return the cooked vegetables to the wok. Stir in the chili paste. Add the rice and the fish sauce; stir-fry for 1 to 2 minutes or till heated through. Arrange the egg strips over the rice mixture. Sprinkle with cilantro or parsley. Garnish with lime wedges. Serve immediately. Makes 4 main-dish or 8 side-dish servings.

Nutrition information per serving: 465 calories, 25 g protein, 46 g carbohydrate, 19 g fat (5 g saturated), 164 mg cholesterol, 758 mg sodium, 399 mg potassium.

CURRY RICE WITH PORK

Serve a side dish of steamed broccoli or French-style green beans to complement the spicy hotness of this main dish.

12 ounces lean boneless pork **or**
    4 medium boneless, skinless
    chicken breast halves
    (12 ounces total)
¼ cup water
2 tablespoons thinly sliced fresh
    lemongrass **or** 1 teaspoon
    finely shredded lemon peel
2 tablespoons fish sauce

1 to 2 teaspoons red curry paste
¼ teaspoon ground turmeric
1 tablespoon cooking oil
1 medium onion, chopped
    (½ cup)
3 cups cooked rice
¼ cup chopped peanuts
    Tomato wedges (optional)

■ Trim fat from pork, if using. Rinse chicken and pat dry, if using. Cut pork or chicken into ¾-inch cubes. Set aside. For sauce, in a small bowl stir together the water, lemongrass or lemon peel, fish sauce, curry paste, and turmeric; set aside.

■ Pour the cooking oil into a wok or large skillet. (Add more oil as necessary during cooking.) Preheat over medium-high heat. Add the onion; stir-fry for 1 minute. Add the pork or chicken. Stir-fry for 2 to 3 minutes more or till no pink remains.

■ Stir sauce. Add the sauce to the mixture in the wok. Cook and stir till boiling; reduce heat. Cover and simmer for 5 minutes to blend flavors. Stir in rice. Gently cook and stir till combined and heated through. Sprinkle with nuts. Serve immediately. If desired, garnish with tomato wedges. Makes 4 servings.

Nutrition information per serving: 447 calories, 25 g protein, 47 g carbohydrate, 17 g fat (4 g saturated), 58 mg cholesterol, 699 mg sodium, 422 mg potassium.

YANG CHOW FRIED RICE

1 tablespoon cooking oil
2 beaten eggs
1 tablespoon cooking oil
2 green onions, thinly sliced
   (¼ cup)
1 4½-ounce can shrimp, rinsed,
   drained, and chopped
½ cup finely chopped fully
   cooked ham or cooked
   chicken

1 7-ounce jar straw mushrooms,
   drained and halved
   lengthwise, or other canned
   mushrooms
3 cups chilled cooked rice
2 tablespoons soy sauce
1 cup shredded lettuce
½ cup frozen peas, thawed

■ Pour 1 tablespoon cooking oil into a wok or large skillet. Preheat over medium heat. Add the eggs. Lift and tilt the wok to form a thin sheet of egg. Cook, without stirring, about 2 minutes or just till set. Slide the egg sheet onto a cutting board. Cut into 2x¾-inch strips. Set aside.

■ Pour 1 tablespoon cooking oil into the wok or skillet. (Add more oil as necessary during cooking.) Preheat over medium-high heat. Add the green onions; stir-fry for 30 seconds. Add the shrimp, ham or chicken, and mushrooms; stir-fry for 1 minute. Stir in the rice and sprinkle with soy sauce. Stir-fry for 1 to 2 minutes more or till heated through. Stir in the egg strips, lettuce, and peas. Heat through. Gently toss. Serve immediately. Makes 6 side-dish servings.

Nutrition information per serving: 261 calories, 14 g protein, 33 g carbohydrate, 8 g fat (1 g saturated), 110 mg cholesterol, 626 mg sodium, 233 mg potassium.

CHINESE SPECIALTY
In China, vendors in roadside stalls and bus stations sell fried rice as a fast-food meal or snack. Sometimes it is served in restaurants, where it accompanies plain rice but never replaces it.

炒
鍋
烹
飪

Sizzling Rice with Shrimp

Sizzling Rice with Shrimp

2 cups cooked rice
12 ounces fresh or frozen peeled and deveined medium shrimp
2 tablespoons soy sauce
4 teaspoons cornstarch
1 tablespoon rice vinegar or white vinegar
2 teaspoons sugar
½ teaspoon instant chicken bouillon granules
    Cooking oil or shortening for deep-fat frying

1 tablespoon cooking oil
1 clove garlic, minced
1 large sweet red or green pepper, cut into ½-inch pieces (1⅓ cups)
4 green onions, bias sliced into ½-inch pieces (¾ cup)
3 medium carrots, thinly sliced into carrot flowers (see directions, page 62) or thinly bias sliced (1½ cups)
2 cups fresh pea pods or one 6-ounce package frozen pea pods, thawed

CHINESE SPECIALTY
The sizzle in the name of this dish comes from the sizzle you hear when the hot shrimp sauce hits the fried rice patties.

■ For rice patties, spread rice into a greased 8x4x2-inch loaf pan. Turn out onto a baking sheet. Bake, uncovered, in a 300° oven for 1½ to 2 hours or till dry. Cool rice and break into 2-inch pieces. Set aside. Thaw shrimp, if frozen. For sauce, in a medium mixing bowl combine the soy sauce, cornstarch, vinegar, sugar, chicken bouillon granules, and 1 cup *water*. Set aside.

■ In a wok or 3-quart saucepan heat 1½ to 2 inches of cooking oil to 365°. Fry rice patties, a few at a time, for 40 to 60 seconds or till light brown and crisp, turning once. Drain on paper towels. Place on a heatproof platter. Keep warm in a 300° oven while preparing shrimp mixture.

■ Pour 1 tablespoon cooking oil into a large skillet. (Add more oil as necessary during cooking.) Preheat over medium-high heat. Stir-fry garlic in hot oil for 15 seconds. Add pepper and onions; stir-fry about 1½ minutes or till crisp-tender. Remove. Add carrots; stir-fry 3 minutes. Add fresh or thawed pea pods; stir-fry about 1 minute or till crisp-tender. Remove. Add shrimp. Stir-fry for 2 to 3 minutes or till shrimp turn pink. Push shrimp from the center. Stir sauce. Add the sauce to the center of the skillet. Cook and stir till thickened and bubbly. Return vegetables to the skillet. Stir all ingredients to coat with sauce. To serve, arrange the fried rice patties on 4 serving plates. Spoon hot shrimp mixture atop. Makes 4 servings.

Nutrition information per serving: 560 calories, 21 g protein, 49 g carbohydrate, 32 g fat (4 g saturated), 125 mg cholesterol, 818 mg sodium, 564 mg potassium.

Oriental Cuisines at a Glance

Chinese

China covers a vast territory and has a diverse cuisine that commonly is divided into regional styles of cooking. Although the regions are alike in many respects, each area has unique distinctions.

Northern cuisine tends to be elegant and mildly seasoned food. Wheat, in the form of noodles, pancakes, and buns, is a staple. Garlic, gingerroot, chives, green onions, and wine are used as seasonings in many foods.

Western cuisine includes the inland provinces. Highly seasoned and spicy hot, the cuisine makes use of hot peppers, green onions, garlic, gingerroot, vinegar, Szechwan peppers, dried mushrooms, and tangerine peel.

Southern cuisine features the Chinese foods Americans know best. Southern China is the home of egg rolls, fried rice, and steamed dumplings. Dishes from this region are characterized by delicate seasonings, the heavy use of sauces, and the natural sweetness of fruits and vegetables.

Eastern cuisine focuses on Shanghai, which is located in one of the richest and most fertile agricultural regions of China. This cuisine is subtle and complex, makes liberal use of sugar and oil, and incorporates brightly colored ingredients. Red-cooking is a specialty of this cuisine.

Japanese

Japanese food provides a feast for the eyes as well as the palate. The Japanese stress seasonal foods prepared simply and then artistically arranged on the plate. Exotic vegetables, tofu, seaweed, and short grain rice are the staples of Japanese cooking.

Korean

Korea's cuisine is strongly flavored and characterized by hearty dishes, soups, and the generous use of beef. Garlic, green onions, soy sauce, gingerroot, pepper, sesame seeds, and sesame oil flavor many foods.

Vietnamese

Vietnamese food reflects the influences of China, India, France, and all of Southeast Asia. Aromatic herbs complement delicately seasoned fresh vegetables, meats, and fish. Fish sauce is a universal seasoning both in cooking and at the table.

Thai

The basic approach to Thai cooking is Chinese in style. However, the Thai love of spices, especially curries and pungent condiments, comes from India. Favorite seasonings include fish sauce, curry powder, lemongrass, shrimp paste, coriander, and chili peppers.

VEGETABLE FRIED RICE

8 dried mushrooms
1 beaten egg
3 tablespoons soy sauce
3 tablespoons rice wine or dry
    white wine
⅛ teaspoon pepper
1 tablespoon cooking oil
1 cup loose-pack frozen green
    beans, thawed and well-
    drained

1 medium stalk celery, bias
    sliced (½ cup)
1 small onion, halved and
    sliced (⅓ cup)
½ of an 8-ounce can bamboo
    shoots, drained
2 cups chilled cooked rice
¼ cup peanut halves

■ In a mixing bowl soak the mushrooms for 30 minutes in enough warm water to cover. Rinse well and squeeze to drain thoroughly. Chop mushrooms, discarding stems. In a small bowl combine the beaten egg, soy sauce, rice wine or white wine, and pepper. Set aside.

■ Pour cooking oil into a wok or large skillet. (Add more oil as necessary during cooking.) Preheat over medium-high heat. Add thawed green beans, celery, and onion; stir-fry for 3 to 4 minutes or till crisp-tender. Remove the vegetables from the wok. Add the mushrooms and bamboo shoots; stir-fry for 1 minute. Return all vegetables to the wok. Add cooked rice. While stirring rice mixture constantly, drizzle egg mixture over rice. Cook and stir for 6 to 8 minutes or till mixture is heated through. Sprinkle with peanut halves. Serve immediately. Makes 4 side-dish servings.

Nutrition information per serving: 290 calories, 9 g protein, 42 g carbohydrate, 10 g fat, (2 g saturated), 53 mg cholesterol, 849 mg sodium, 382 mg potassium.

CHINESE SPECIALTY
When making fried rice, be sure to start with thoroughly chilled, cooked rice. During chilling much of the moisture in the rice evaporates. This allows the oil to coat the grains during stir-frying to keep them from sticking together.

炒鍋烹飪

PORK AND CRAB CHOW MEIN

CHINESE SPECIALTY

Chow mein literally means fried noodles. Chinese typically prepare it using leftovers. So if you don't have one of the ingredients in our recipe, substitute another similar ingredient.

6 ounces steamed or *fresh Chinese egg noodles* or *4 ounces dried Chinese egg noodles*
¼ cup water
2 tablespoons soy sauce
1 teaspoon cornstarch
½ teaspoon sesame oil
¼ teaspoon crushed red pepper
Cooking oil or shortening for deep-fat frying
1 tablespoon cooking oil
2 green onions, sliced (¼ cup)

1½ teaspoons grated gingerroot
3 cloves garlic, minced
2 cups shredded Chinese cabbage or cabbage
1 medium stalk celery, sliced (½ cup)
2 cups shredded, cooked pork, beef, or chicken
1 8-ounce can bamboo shoots, drained
1 6½-ounce can crabmeat, drained, flaked, and cartilage removed

■ In a large saucepan cook noodles in boiling lightly salted water for 4 to 6 minutes or till tender. Drain. Spread noodles on paper towels and let dry at least 30 minutes.

■ For sauce, in a small bowl stir together the water, soy sauce, cornstarch, sesame oil, and red pepper; set aside. In a wok or 3-quart saucepan heat 1½ to 2 inches of cooking oil or shortening to 365°. Fry noodles, about ½ cup at a time, in the hot oil about 1 minute or till golden and crisp. Using a wire-mesh strainer or slotted spoon, remove noodles from oil. Drain on paper towels. Set aside.

■ Pour the 1 tablespoon cooking oil into a 12-inch skillet. (Add more oil as necessary during cooking.) Preheat over medium-high heat. Stir-fry green onions, gingerroot, and garlic in hot oil for 15 seconds. Add regular cabbage (if using) and celery; stir-fry 2 to 3 minutes or till crisp-tender.

■ Stir in the cooked pork, beef, or chicken; bamboo shoots; and crabmeat. Push mixture from the center of the skillet. Stir sauce. Add the sauce to the center of the skillet. Cook and stir till thickened and bubbly. Stir all ingredients together to coat with sauce. Cook and stir about 1 minute more or till heated through. Fold in fried noodles and, if using, Chinese cabbage. Serve immediately. Makes 4 servings.

Nutrition information per serving: 449 calories, 31 g protein, 17 g carbohydrate, 29 g fat (6 g saturated), 109 mg cholesterol, 707 mg sodium, 636 mg potassium.

SESAME CHICKEN AND BEAN THREADS

*1 tablespoon cooking oil
   (optional)*
2 beaten eggs (optional)
*4 medium boneless, skinless
   chicken breast halves
   (12 ounces total)*
¼ cup soy sauce
3 tablespoons water
1 green onion, thinly sliced
1 tablespoon sugar
*1 tablespoon sesame seed,
   crushed*

2 teaspoons sesame oil
2 cloves garlic, minced
8 dried mushrooms
2 ounces bean threads
1 tablespoon cooking oil
*1 small onion, thinly sliced and
   separated into rings*
*1 9-ounce package frozen
   French-style green beans,
   thawed*
2 large carrots, shredded

■ If desired, make egg strips. For egg strips, pour 1 tablespoon cooking oil into a wok or large skillet. Preheat over medium heat. Add eggs. Lift and tilt to form a thin sheet. Cook, without stirring, about 2 minutes or just till set. Slide onto a cutting board. Cut into 2x¾-inch strips. Set aside. Rinse chicken and pat dry. Cut into bite-size strips. For marinade, stir together the soy sauce, water, green onion, sugar, sesame seed, sesame oil, and garlic. Stir in chicken. Cover and marinate for 30 minutes. Drain, reserving marinade.

■ Meanwhile, soak mushrooms for 30 minutes in enough warm water to cover. Rinse and squeeze to drain thoroughly. Slice thinly, discarding stems. Soak bean threads for 15 minutes in enough warm water to cover. Drain well. Cut into 3- to 4-inch lengths. Set aside.

■ Pour 1 tablespoon cooking oil into a wok or large skillet. (Add more oil as necessary during cooking.) Preheat over medium-high heat. Add onion; stir-fry for 2 minutes. Add green beans. Stir-fry for 1 to 2 minutes or till crisp-tender. Add carrots; stir-fry for 30 seconds more or till heated through. Remove the vegetables from the wok. Add the chicken to the hot wok. Stir-fry for 2 to 3 minutes or till no pink remains. Add the reserved marinade, mushrooms, bean threads, and cooked vegetables to the wok. Cook and stir about 1 minute more or till heated through. If desired, garnish with egg strips. Serve immediately. Makes 4 servings.

Nutrition information per serving: 306 calories, 27 g protein, 29 g carbohydrate, 10 g fat (2 g saturated), 54 mg cholesterol, 1,103 mg sodium, 681 mg potassium.

SPICY PORK AND RICE STICKS

For a fancier garnish, add thin slices of fresh red chili pepper to your green onion brush.

3 ounces rice sticks
1 pound lean ground pork
   or beef
2 tablespoons soy sauce
1 teaspoon sesame oil
1 tablespoon cooking oil
   or peanut oil
1 teaspoon purchased chili oil
   or Chili Oil (see recipe,
   page 82)
2 cloves garlic, minced
2 teaspoons grated gingerroot

2 medium carrots, thinly sliced
   into carrot flowers (see
   directions, page 64) or
   thinly bias sliced (1 cup)
4 green onions, cut into 1-inch
   pieces (¾ cup)
2 medium stalks celery, thinly
   bias sliced (1 cup)
½ cup chicken broth
   Onion Brush (see directions,
   page 198)(optional)

■ In a mixing bowl soak rice sticks for 15 minutes in enough warm water to cover. Drain well. Cut into 2- to 3-inch lengths. Set aside. In another bowl combine ground pork or beef, soy sauce, and sesame oil; mix well. Let meat mixture stand for 20 minutes.

■ Pour cooking or peanut oil and chili oil into a wok or large skillet. (Add more cooking oil as necessary during cooking.) Preheat over medium-high heat. Stir-fry the garlic and gingerroot in hot oil for 15 seconds. Add the carrots and green onions; stir-fry for 2 minutes. Add the celery; stir-fry for 2 minutes more or till vegetables are crisp-tender. Remove the vegetables from the wok.

■ Add *half* of the meat mixture to the hot wok. Stir-fry for 2 to 3 minutes or till no pink remains, breaking meat up into small pieces. Remove the meat from the wok. Repeat with remaining meat mixture. Drain off fat. Wipe out wok with paper towels.

■ Return all meat to the wok. Add soaked rice sticks and the cooked vegetables; stir-fry for 1 minute. Add chicken broth. Cook and stir about 1 minute more or till heated through. Serve immediately. If desired, garnish with an Onion Brush. Makes 4 servings.

Nutrition information per serving: 362 calories, 29 g protein, 25 g carbohydrate, 16 g fat, (4 g saturated), 89 mg cholesterol, 734 mg sodium, 662 mg potassium.

Spicy Pork and Rice Sticks

HOMEMADE INGREDIENTS

CHILI OIL
In a small saucepan heat ⅓ cup *cooking oil* and 2 tablespoons *sesame oil* to 365°. Remove from heat. Stir in 2 tablespoons ground *red pepper*. Cool. Strain. Cover and store in the refrigerator. Makes about ½ cup.

Note: For milder flavor, increase *cooking oil* to ½ cup.

DRIED TANGERINE PEEL
Using a vegetable peeler, thinly slice peel from 3 *tangerines or oranges;* cut into 1½ x 1-inch pieces. Scrape off excess white membrane. Place pieces in a single layer on a baking sheet. Bake in a 300° oven for 10 to 12 minutes or till peel is dried. Cool thoroughly. Store in a covered container. Makes about ⅓ cup peel.

FIVE-SPICE POWDER
In a blender container combine 3 tablespoons ground *cinnamon;* 6 *star anise or* 2 teaspoons *aniseed;* 1½ teaspoons *fennel seed;* 1½ teaspoons whole *Szechwan peppers or* whole *black peppers;* and ¾ teaspoon ground *cloves.* Cover and blend to a fine powder. Store in a tightly covered container. Makes about ⅓ cup.

PLUM SAUCE
In a small saucepan combine one 12-ounce jar *plum preserves or plum jam* (about 1 cup); 2 tablespoons *vinegar;* 1 tablespoon *brown sugar;* 1 tablespoon finely chopped *onion;* 1 teaspoon seeded and finely chopped dried *red chili pepper or* 1 teaspoon crushed *red pepper;* 1 clove *garlic,* minced; and ½ teaspoon ground *ginger.* Bring to boiling, stirring constantly. Remove from heat; cover and cool. Store in a tightly covered container in the refrigerator. Makes 1¼ cups.

ROASTED SALT AND PEPPER
Spray a *cold* wok or large skillet with *nonstick spray coating.* Preheat over medium heat. Add ¼ cup coarse *kosher salt* and ¼ cup whole *Szechwan peppers or* whole *black peppers.* Stir-fry for 5 to 7 minutes or till the whole peppers begin to pop and smoke. Remove the wok from the heat. Let the mixture cool to room temperature. Grind the mixture in a food processor, clean coffee grinder, or with a mortar and pestle. Store in a tightly covered container. Makes about ½ cup.

SZECHWAN CHICKEN-PASTA SALAD

4 large boneless, skinless chicken
   breast halves (1 pound
   total)
2 cups fresh pea pods or one
   6-ounce package frozen pea
   pods, thawed
¼ cup soy sauce
2 tablespoons rice vinegar or
   white vinegar
1 teaspoon purchased chili oil
   or Chili Oil (see recipe,
   page 82)
¼ to ½ teaspoon crushed red
   pepper

8 ounces steamed or *fresh*
   Chinese egg noodles or
   5 ounces dried Chinese
   egg noodles
1 tablespoon cooking oil
2 cloves garlic, minced
1 large sweet red or green
   pepper, cut into thin strips
   (1⅓ cups)
2 green onions, sliced (¼ cup)
¼ cup coarsely chopped peanuts

*To make this a truly
international dish,
substitute linguine or
spaghetti for the
Chinese egg noodles.
Just break 7 ounces of
uncooked pasta into
3- to 4-inch lengths
and cook it according
to package directions.
(Pictured on pages
68 and 69.)*

■ Rinse chicken and pat dry. Cut into ¾-inch pieces. Coarsely chop the pea pods. For sauce, in a small bowl stir together the soy sauce, rice vinegar or white vinegar, chili oil, and crushed red pepper. Set aside.

■ In a large saucepan cook noodles in boiling lightly salted water for 4 to 6 minutes or till tender. Drain. Set aside.

■ Pour cooking oil into a wok or large skillet. (Add more oil as necessary during cooking.) Stir-fry the garlic in hot oil for 15 seconds. Add the pea pods, red or green pepper, and green onions; stir-fry for 1 to 2 minutes or till crisp-tender. Remove the vegetables from the wok.

■ Add *half* of the chicken to the hot wok. Stir-fry for 2 to 3 minutes or till no pink remains. Remove the chicken from the wok. Repeat with remaining chicken. Return all chicken to the wok. Add the sauce to the wok. Add the cooked vegetables and noodles. Stir ingredients together to coat with sauce. Cook and stir about 1 minute more or till heated through. Sprinkle with peanuts. Serve immediately. Makes 5 servings.

Nutrition information per serving: 295 calories, 28 g protein, 21 g carbohydrate, 11 g fat (2 g saturated), 72 mg cholesterol, 914 mg sodium, 438 mg potassium.

THAI CHICKEN AND CRISPY NOODLES

炒
餉
烹
飪

THAI SPECIALTY
The Chinese invented crisp fried noodles, but the Thai embellished them. Thai usually cook this dish with what's available in the family pantry, but it always contains seafood and meat or poultry mingled with a sweet-and-sour sauce.

4 medium boneless, skinless
   chicken breast halves
   (12 ounces total)
8 ounces fresh **or** frozen peeled
   and deveined shrimp
6 dried mushrooms
2 dried wood ears (optional)
2 tablespoons rice vinegar
   or white vinegar
1 tablespoon sugar

1 tablespoon fish sauce
2 teaspoons soy sauce
¼ teaspoon crushed red pepper
1 tablespoon cooking oil
1 medium onion, chopped
   (½ cup)
   Fried Rice Sticks (see recipe,
   page 86)
1 tablespoon snipped cilantro
   or parsley

■ Rinse chicken and pat dry. Cut into thin bite-size pieces. Set aside. Thaw shrimp, if frozen. Halve shrimp lengthwise; set aside.

■ In a mixing bowl soak the mushrooms and, if desired, wood ears for 30 minutes in enough warm water to cover. Rinse well and squeeze to drain thoroughly. Slice thinly, discarding stems. Set aside.

■ In a small bowl stir together the rice vinegar or white vinegar, sugar, fish sauce, soy sauce, and red pepper, stirring to dissolve sugar. Set aside.

■ Pour cooking oil into a wok or large skillet. (Add more oil as necessary during cooking.) Preheat over medium-high heat. Stir-fry the onion in hot oil for 1 minute. Add the chicken. Stir-fry for 2 to 3 minutes or till no pink remains. Remove the chicken and onion from wok. Add the shrimp to the wok. Stir-fry for 2 to 3 minutes or till shrimp turn pink. Stir in the mushrooms, wood ears (if desired), chicken-onion mixture, and vinegar mixture. Cook and stir about 1 minute or till heated through. Stir in *half* of the Fried Rice Sticks, tossing to coat but being careful not to break up rice sticks. Sprinkle with cilantro or parsley. Serve immediately over remaining Fried Rice Sticks. Makes 4 servings.

Nutrition information per serving: 386 calories, 32 g protein, 32 g carbohydrate, 14 g fat (2 g saturated), 137 mg cholesterol, 625 mg sodium, 400 mg potassium.

PRECIOUS-TREASURES PUDDING

2 cups water
1 cup short grain rice
¼ cup sugar
1 tablespoon cooking oil,
    margarine, or butter
½ cup red and/or green candied
    cherries, halved

¼ cup chopped candied orange
    peel
¼ cup slivered almonds
¼ cup raisins
½ cup sweet red bean paste
    Lemon Glaze

■ In a medium saucepan combine the water and rice. Heat to boiling. Reduce heat. Cover and simmer for 15 to 20 minutes or till water is absorbed. Stir in the sugar and oil, margarine, or butter. Set aside.

■ Arrange the candied cherries, the candied orange peel, almonds, and raisins in a decorative pattern on the bottom and partially up the sides of a well-greased 1-quart casserole or a 1-quart heatproof bowl or mold.

■ Spoon *half* of the rice mixture into the casserole, being careful not to displace the fruit and nuts. Make a well in the center of the rice, leaving the rice about ½ inch thick on the sides.

■ Spoon red bean paste into the depression, spreading evenly. Spoon remaining rice mixture on top of bean paste. Press lightly with the back of a spoon that has been dipped in water. Cover casserole tightly with foil. In a wok, place a steamer rack over water. Bring water to boiling over high heat. Place casserole on the rack. Cover and steam for 45 minutes. Carefully unmold onto a serving platter. Serve warm with Lemon Glaze. Serves 6.

NOTE: If sweet red bean paste is unavailable, substitute ½ cup *date cake and pastry filling*.

LEMON GLAZE: In a small saucepan stir together ¼ cup *sugar* and 1 tablespoon *cornstarch*. Stir in ⅔ cup *water* and 2 tablespoons *lemon juice*. Cook and stir till thickened and bubbly. Cook and stir for 2 minutes more. Stir in 1 tablespoon *margarine or butter* and 1 teaspoon finely shredded *lemon peel*.

Nutrition information per serving: 404 calories, 4 g protein, 82 g carbohydrate, 8 g fat (1 g saturated), 00 mg cholesterol, 52 mg sodium, 137 mg potassium.

CHINESE SPECIALTY
The treasures are the fruits traditionally used in the Orient to decorate the pudding—dates, papaya, kumquats, lotus seeds, litchis, longans, ginkgo nuts, and candied ginger. Our recipe uses fruits more readily available to Americans.

Attractively arrange the fruits and nuts on the bottom and partially up the sides of a well-greased casserole. Greasing helps hold the fruits in place and keeps the rice from sticking to the sides of the dish.

BASIC RICE

2 cups water
1 cup long grain rice

¼ teaspoon salt

■ In a wok or medium saucepan combine water, rice, and salt. Bring to boiling. Reduce heat; cover and simmer for 15 minutes. Do not lift cover. Remove from heat. Let stand, covered, for 10 minutes. Makes 4 servings.

OVEN RICE: Prepare as directed above, *except* substitute *2¼ cups boiling water* for the 2 cups water and combine the ingredients in a 1-quart casserole. Cover and bake in a 350° oven about 35 minutes or till rice is tender. Fluff rice with a fork after 20 minutes. Makes 4 servings.

MICROWAVE RICE: Prepare as directed above, *except* combine the ingredients in a 2-quart microwave-safe casserole. Micro-cook, uncovered, on 100% power (high) about 6 minutes or till boiling. Stir, then cover. Cook for 5 minutes more; stir. Cook, covered, for 3 minutes more. Stir. Cover and let stand for 5 to 10 minutes. Makes 4 servings.

Nutrition information per serving: 169 calories, 3 g protein, 37 g carbohydrate, 0 g fat (0 g saturated), 0 mg cholesterol, 136 mg sodium, 53 mg potassium.

FRIED BEAN THREADS OR RICE STICKS

Cooking oil or *shortening for*
deep-fat frying

3 ounces bean threads or
4 ounces rice sticks

■ In a wok or 3-quart saucepan heat 1½ to 2 inches of cooking oil to 375°. Fry bean threads or rice sticks, a few at a time, in the hot oil about 5 seconds or till they puff and rise to the top. Using a wire strainer or slotted spoon, remove bean threads or rice sticks from oil. Drain on paper towels. If desired, keep warm in a 300° oven. Makes 4 servings.

Nutrition information per serving: 133 calories, 5 g protein, 13 g carbohydrate, 7 g fat (1 g saturated), 00 mg cholesterol, 1 mg sodium, 219 mg potassium.

NOODLE CAKE

*6 ounces steamed or fresh
  Chinese egg noodles or
  4 ounces dried Chinese egg
  noodles*

1 tablespoon cooking oil

■ If necessary, cut or break noodles into 4- to 5-inch lengths. In a large saucepan cook noodles in boiling lightly salted water for 4 to 6 minutes or till tender. Drain and rinse with cold water to cool; drain well.

■ Pour oil into a heavy nonstick or well-seasoned skillet. Heat over medium heat. Lift and tilt the skillet to coat sides with oil. With a pancake turner, pat noodles into the skillet.

■ Cook, uncovered, over medium heat for 5 to 6 minutes or till bottom of noodle cake is lightly browned. Loosen noodle cake with a large spatula, then carefully invert the skillet and noodle cake onto a baking sheet or a large plate.

■ Slide noodle cake back into the skillet, brown side up. Cook, uncovered, for 5 to 6 minutes more or till bottom is lightly browned. Remove from heat. Loosen from pan and transfer to a serving platter. Makes 4 servings.

Nutrition information per serving: 87 calories, 2 g protein, 11 g carbohydrate, 4 g fat, (1 g saturated),13 mg cholesterol, 3 mg sodium, 12 mg potassium.

INDIVIDUAL NOODLE CAKES: Prepare as directed above, *except* omit the cooking oil. To make 8 noodle cakes, place a generous ¼ cup of cooked noodles onto a greased baking sheet for each noodle cake. Shape noodles into patties about 4 inches in diameter. Bake in a 400° oven for 15 to 20 minutes or till tops are crisp and lightly browned. Makes 4 servings.

OVEN NOODLE CAKE: Prepare as directed above, *except* omit the cooking oil. Spread cooked noodles in a greased 9x1½-inch round baking pan. Bake in a 400° oven for 20 to 25 minutes or till top is crisp and lightly browned. Transfer to a serving platter. Makes 4 servings.

Nutrition information per serving: 57 calories, 2 g protein, 11 g carbohydrate, 1 g fat (0 g saturated), 13 mg cholesterol, 3 mg sodium, 12 mg potassium.

Traditionally, Oriental cooks toss the noodle patty in the air and hope that it will land, a split second later, back in the pan. We found it easier to invert the cake onto a baking sheet or plate, then slide it back into the pan.

Frying

The crispness and flavors of fried specialties from the Orient are characteristics Americans have come to love. Here you'll find a treasury of traditional fried dishes, such as Japanese Tempura, Chinese Cantonese Lemon Chicken, and Vietnamese Fried Stuffed Bananas.

Sesame Puffs
(see recipe, page 109)

With a wok and a little know-how, you can fry restaurant specialties like egg rolls and sweet-and-sour pork right in your own home. Glance through "The Frying Workshop" and discover numerous tips to help make frying foods both safe and successful.

THE FRYING WORKSHOP

Even though you may not think of using your wok for deep-fat frying, it works well for that purpose. Its large surface area allows foods to float freely in the cooking oil or melted shortening and its unique shape requires less oil than most pans or deep-fat fryers.

EQUIPMENT FOR FRYING

■ Any type of wok will work for frying foods, but a flat-bottom wok is the most stable and this reduces the chances of tipping and spilling. If you want to use a round-bottom wok, make sure the ring stand is sturdy and the wok sits in it tightly. If you don't own a wok or are using it for another part of your meal, use a 3-quart saucepan for frying.

■ A deep-fat frying thermometer helps you monitor the proper frying temperature. Use a long flat thermometer like the one pictured on page 10. Or, use any deep-fat frying thermometer that will clip on the side of the wok with its bulb in the oil but not touching the pan itself. Candy thermometers that register up to 400° can double as deep-fat frying thermometers.

■ Use a wire-mesh strainer or a slotted spoon with a long handle to remove food from the hot oil. They let the oil drain off, allowing you to remove just the food. If you don't

have a wire-mesh strainer or slotted spoon, use wooden or metal tongs. When using tongs, it is important to work quickly because you can only remove one piece of food at a time.

■ Drain fried foods on a wok rack or on several layers of paper towels. Some woks come with a semi-circular or doughnut-shape wire rack that fits over the edges of the wok, allowing the excess fat from the food to drip back into the wok.

GUIDES TO GOOD FRYING

1. As always, when cooking with hot oil, safety is important. Be sure your wok or pan is stable before you add the oil or shortening to it. After the oil is heated, you don't want any hot oil spills.

The best oil for frying is a clear, relatively flavorless oil that can be heated to a very high temperature without smoking. Although peanut oil is favored by many Oriental cooks, corn, cottonseed, and other vegetable oils work just as well.

When you add the oil to your wok or 3-quart saucepan, measure at the deepest point. An adequate amount of oil or melted shortening for frying most foods is 1½ to 2 inches (about 4 cups). This amount allows enough room to add the food.

2. For perfectly fried foods, it is critical to keep the oil at the correct temperature. Maintaining a constant oil temperature produces food that is moist inside and golden outside. Oil that is too hot burns the outside of the food and leaves the inside underdone. On the other hand, oil that is not hot enough cooks food more slowly and causes the food to retain more grease.

Before cooking, heat the oil to the temperature indicated in the recipe; in most cases it's 365° or 375°. Use a deep-fat frying thermometer to help take the guesswork out of monitoring the frying temperature.

Even with electric woks, which have thermostats, you'll need to use a thermometer to monitor the temperature. As the thermostat cycles on and off, the temperature can fluctuate several degrees.

3. When frying foods, make sure the pieces are uniform in size. Foods the same size cook in approximately the same amount of time. Also, be sure to add just a few pieces of food at a time to the hot oil. Too much food in the hot oil at one time will lower its temperature and the food will take longer to cook.

To minimize splattering, gently lower the food into the oil using a

wire-mesh strainer or slotted spoon, as shown. This helps reduce the chance of burning your hands.

4. When the food is done, use a wire-mesh strainer or slotted spoon to remove it from the hot oil. To drain, place the food on a wok rack or paper towels. If you have more food to fry, place the cooked food in a baking pan and keep it warm in a 300° oven till serving time.

Between batches of frying, allow the oil to reheat to its original temperature. Also, skim away bits of food that may have broken off during frying before they have a chance to burn.

REUSING OIL
For fresh flavor in fried foods, use new cooking oil or shortening. However, if you wish to reuse the cooking oil or shortening after it's been used once, allow it to cool enough to handle safely.

For *cooking oil,* strain it through a paper coffee filter set in a metal strainer or through a double thickness of 100 percent cotton cheesecloth. Refrigerate strained oil in a covered jar and use within a few days. When you reuse the oil, *add an equal amount* of fresh oil to help avoid smoking and possible flare-ups.

For *shortening,* strain as directed for oil. Then, refrigerate it in a covered container and use within a few days. When you reuse shortening, it's not necessary to add an equal amount of fresh shortening.

FRIED ZUCCHINI APPETIZERS

KOREAN SPECIALTY

Although sweet potatoes aren't traditionally used in this appetizer, they make a tasty alternative to zucchini. If you want to use sweet potatoes, choose small ones that are about 1½ inches in diameter.

3 medium zucchini *or* 3 small sweet potatoes
1 slightly beaten egg
1 pound ground raw chicken *or* ground raw turkey (2 cups)
2 tablespoons finely chopped onion
1 clove garlic, minced
1 teaspoon sesame oil
1 teaspoon sesame seed
Dash salt

Dash pepper
Cooking oil *or* shortening for deep-fat frying
1 slightly beaten egg
1 cup all-purpose flour
1 cup ice water
2 tablespoons cooking oil
½ teaspoon sugar
½ teaspoon salt
2 ice cubes
Soy sauce (optional)

■ Slice the zucchini into ½-inch-thick slices or slice the sweet potatoes into ¼-inch-thick slices. Combine 1 egg, chicken or turkey, onion, garlic, sesame oil, sesame seed, the dash of salt, and the pepper. Sprinkle each side of the zucchini or sweet potato slices with additional salt and pepper. Spread one side of *each* zucchini or sweet potato slice with about *2 teaspoons* of the chicken or turkey mixture.

■ In a wok or 3-quart saucepan heat 1½ to 2 inches of cooking oil or shortening to 365°. Meanwhile, for batter, in a mixing bowl combine 1 egg, flour, ice water, the 2 tablespoons oil, sugar, and the ½ teaspoon salt. Mix just till moistened (a few lumps should remain). Stir in the ice cubes. Use the batter at once.

■ Dip the zucchini slices in batter, swirling to coat. Allow excess batter to drip off. Fry, a few at a time, in hot oil for 3 to 4 minutes or till light brown, turning slices once. Using a wire strainer or slotted spoon, remove food from the oil. Drain on a wok rack or on paper towels. Keep warm in a 300° oven while frying the remaining slices. Serve warm. If desired, pass soy sauce. Makes 8 appetizer servings.

Nutrition information per serving: 446 calories, 17 g protein, 15 g carbohydrate, 36 g fat (5 g saturated), 91 mg cholesterol, 203 mg sodium, 301 mg potassium.

PHOENIX-TAILED SHRIMP

1 pound fresh or frozen large
   shrimp
2 tablespoons dry sherry
½ teaspoon grated gingerroot
   Cooking oil or shortening for
   deep-fat frying
¾ cup all-purpose flour
1 green onion, finely chopped
   (2 tablespoons)

1½ teaspoons baking powder
¼ teaspoon salt
¼ teaspoon grated gingerroot
⅔ cup water
   Sweet-and-Sour Dipping
   Sauce (see recipe, page 112)
   (optional)

CHINESE SPECIALTY
Skip the chopsticks! The Chinese tradition-ally eat these shrimp with their fingers. Just grasp the fanned tail and enjoy.

■ Thaw shrimp, if frozen. Peel and devein shrimp. Using a sharp knife, carefully slit the shrimp all along its inner curve, cutting just three-fourths of the way through the flesh. *Do not* cut through tail. Turn the shrimp cut side down. Using the flat side of a meat mallet, slightly flatten the shrimp. Stir together the sherry and the ½ teaspoon gingerroot. Toss with the shrimp. Cover and let stand while preparing oil and batter.

■ In a wok or 3-quart saucepan heat 1½ to 2 inches cooking oil or shorten-ing to 365°. Meanwhile, for batter, in a small mixing bowl combine the flour, green onion, baking powder, salt, and the ¼ teaspoon grated ginger-root. Add the water. Using a rotary beater or wire whisk, beat till smooth.

■ Pick up each shrimp by the tail. Dip all but the tip of the tail into the batter, swirling to coat. Fry shrimp, a few at a time, in the hot oil about 3 minutes or till golden, turning once. Using a wire strainer or slotted spoon, remove shrimp from oil. Drain on a wok rack or on paper towels. Keep warm in a 300° oven while frying remaining shrimp. If desired, serve shrimp with Sweet-and-Sour Dipping Sauce. Makes 12 appetizer servings.

Nutrition information per serving: 261 calories, 7 g protein, 16 g carbohydrate, 19 g fat (2 g saturated), 55 mg cholesterol, 258 mg sodium, 116 mg potassium.

Use a sharp knife and cut the shrimp lengthwise along the inner curve, cutting just three-fourths of the way through the flesh. Leave the tail intact, because it fans out and makes a great handle for dipping.

EGG ROLL WRAPPING

1 *Place an egg roll wrapper with a point toward you. Spoon about ¼ cup of the desired filling (see recipes, pages 95, 97, and 99) across and just below the center of the egg roll wrapper. Fold the bottom point of the egg roll wrapper over the filling. Then tuck it under the filling, as shown.*

2 *Fold the side corners of the egg roll wrapper over the filling, forming an envelope shape, as shown.*

3 *Roll the egg roll toward the remaining corner. Moisten the top point and press firmly to seal.*

VEGETABLE FILLING

8 *dried mushrooms*
8 *ounces firm tofu*
1 *tablespoon water*
1 *tablespoon soy sauce*
1 *teaspoon cornstarch*
1 *teaspoon sugar*
½ *teaspoon sesame oil*
1 *tablespoon cooking oil*
2 *cloves garlic, minced*
4 *cups finely shredded Chinese*
   cabbage **or** *cabbage*

2 *medium carrots, shredded*
   (1 cup)
Cooking oil **or** *shortening*
   for deep-fat frying
10 *egg roll wrappers* **or**
   60 wonton wrappers
Chinese Mustard Sauce
   (see recipe, page 113)
or *Chili Dipping Sauce*
   (see recipe, page 112)

■ In a mixing bowl soak dried mushrooms for 30 minutes in enough warm water to cover. Rinse well and squeeze to drain thoroughly. Chop finely, discarding stems. Set aside. Cut tofu into ¼-inch cubes. In a bowl stir together the water, soy sauce, cornstarch, sugar, and sesame oil.

■ Pour the 1 tablespoon cooking oil into a large skillet. (Add more oil as necessary during cooking.) Preheat over medium-high heat. Stir-fry garlic in hot oil for 15 seconds. Add the regular cabbage (if using) and stir-fry for 1 minute. Add the carrots and stir-fry for 1 minute. Stir the soy mixture. Add to the skillet. Cook and stir till thickened and bubbly. Cook and stir 1 minute more. Stir in the mushrooms, tofu, and, if using, Chinese cabbage. Remove from skillet and cool.

■ In a wok or 3-quart saucepan heat 1½ to 2 inches of cooking oil or shortening to 365°. Fill egg roll wrappers or wonton wrappers as directed on page 94 or 98.

■ Fry egg rolls or wontons, a few at a time, in the hot oil for 1 to 2½ minutes or till golden, turning once. Using a wire strainer or slotted spoon, remove food from oil. Drain on a wok rack or on paper towels. Keep warm in a 300° oven while frying remaining food. Serve warm with Chinese Mustard Sauce or Chili Dipping Sauce. Makes 10 appetizer servings.

Nutrition information per serving: 191 calories, 4 g protein, 11 g carbohydrate, 15 g fat (2 g saturated), 0 mg cholesterol, 251 mg sodium, 197 mg potassium.

CHINESE SPECIALTY

Egg rolls and wontons, the Chinese delicacies that Westerners know best, originated in the region around Canton.

In the mid-19th century, the Cantonese emigrated in large numbers from China. Thus, egg rolls and wontons were among the first Oriental foods served beyond China's borders.

炒鍋烹飪

CRAB AND CREAM CHEESE FILLING

1 6-ounce can crabmeat, drained, flaked, and cartilage removed
½ of an 8-ounce package cream cheese, softened
1 tablespoon snipped chives or sliced green onion

Cooking oil or shortening for deep-fat frying
30 wonton wrappers
Plum Sauce (see recipe, page 82) or Sweet-and-Sour Dipping Sauce (see recipe, page 112)

■ In a mixing bowl combine the crabmeat, cream cheese, and chives or green onion. In a wok or 3-quart saucepan heat 1½ to 2 inches of cooking oil or shortening to 365°. Fill wonton wrappers as directed on page 98. Fry wontons, a few at a time, in hot oil for 1 to 2½ minutes or till golden, turning once. Using a wire strainer or slotted spoon, remove food from oil. Drain on a wok rack or on paper towels. Keep warm in a 300° oven while frying remaining wontons.

■ Serve warm with Plum Sauce or Sweet-and-Sour Dipping Sauce. Makes 10 appetizer servings.

Nutrition information per serving: 177 calories, 5 g protein, 17 g carbohydrate, 10 g fat (3 g saturated), 25 mg cholesterol, 295 mg sodium, 127 mg potassium.

WRAPPING IT UP

Egg roll wrappers (sometimes called egg roll skins) and wonton wrappers both are thin sheets of noodle dough used for fried and steamed Oriental specialties. Most supermarkets or Oriental grocery stores sell them either refrigerated or frozen.

Egg roll wrappers are available square or round and regular or thin. The shape doesn't matter—they both work well in our recipes. The thinner egg roll wrappers make slightly flakier fried pastries than the regular ones, but you can use either kind.

GROUND MEAT FILLING

2 tablespoons water
1 tablespoon dry sherry
1 tablespoon soy sauce
½ teaspoon cornstarch
⅛ teaspoon ground red pepper
⅛ teaspoon pepper
1 tablespoon cooking oil
2 cloves garlic, minced
2 teaspoons grated gingerroot
2 cups finely chopped Chinese cabbage or cabbage
4 green onions, thinly sliced (½ cup)
8 ounces lean ground beef or pork

1 4-ounce can mushroom stems and pieces, drained and finely chopped
Cooking oil or shortening for deep-fat frying
12 egg roll wrappers or 72 wonton wrappers
Sweet-and-Sour Dipping Sauce (see recipe, page 112), Chili Dipping Sauce (see recipe, page 112), or Chinese Mustard Sauce (see recipe, page 113)

This filling incorporates an American favorite—ground beef. The meat is combined with Oriental seasonings, making the filling taste just as Chinese as any other filling.

■ For sauce, stir together the water, sherry, soy sauce, cornstarch, red pepper, and pepper. Set aside. Pour the 1 tablespoon oil into a large skillet. (Add more oil as necessary during cooking.) Preheat over medium-high heat. Stir-fry garlic and gingerroot in hot oil for 15 seconds. Add regular cabbage (if using) and green onions. Stir-fry for 1½ to 2½ minutes or till crisp-tender. Remove vegetables. Add the ground beef or pork; stir-fry for 2 to 3 minutes or till no pink remains. Drain off fat. Push meat from the center of the skillet. Stir sauce. Add sauce to the center of the skillet. Cook and stir till thickened and bubbly. Add cooked vegetables, mushrooms, and, if using, Chinese cabbage. Stir all ingredients together to coat with sauce. Cook and stir about 1 minute more or till heated through. Remove from skillet; cool.

■ In a wok or 3-quart saucepan heat 1½ to 2 inches of cooking oil or shortening to 365°. Meanwhile, fill wrappers as directed on page 94 or 98. Fry egg rolls or wontons, a few at a time, in hot oil for 1 to 2½ minutes or till golden brown, turning once. Remove from oil. Drain on a wok rack or on paper towels. Keep warm in a 300° oven while frying remaining food. Serve warm with Sweet-and-Sour Dipping Sauce, Chili Dipping Sauce, or Chinese Mustard Sauce. Makes 12 appetizer servings.

Nutrition information per serving: 210 calories, 6 g protein, 16 g carbohydrate, 14 g fat (2 g saturated), 15 mg cholesterol, 307 mg sodium, 156 mg potassium.

WONTON WRAPPING

1 *Place the wonton wrapper with a point toward you. Spoon 2 teaspoonfuls of the desired filling (see recipes, pages 95, 96, 97, and 99) just below the center. Fold the bottom point over the filling. Then tuck it under the filling, as shown.*

2 *Roll the wonton wrapper once to cover the filling, leaving about 1 inch unrolled at the top of the wrapper, as shown. Moisten the right-hand corner of the wrapper with a little water.*

3 *Grasp the right- and left-hand corners of the wrapper. Bring these corners toward you, below the filling, as shown. Overlap the left-hand and the right-hand corners. Press the corners together securely to seal.*

PORK AND SHRIMP FILLING

8 dried mushrooms
1 ounce bean threads
8 ounces fresh or frozen peeled
    and deveined shrimp
8 ounces lean boneless pork
2 tablespoons water
2 tablespoons oyster sauce
1 tablespoon rice wine
2 teaspoons cornstarch
1 tablespoon cooking oil
1 tablespoon grated gingerroot
2 cloves garlic, minced
1 medium carrot, finely
    shredded

½ cup fresh bean sprouts,
    chopped
2 green onions, sliced
    Cooking oil or shortening
    for deep-fat frying
16 egg roll wrappers or
    96 wonton wrappers
    Sweet-and-Sour Dipping
    Sauce (see recipe, page
    112), Honey Dipping Sauce
    (see recipe, page 113),
    or Chinese Mustard Sauce
    (see recipe, page 113)

CHINESE SPECIALTY
Originally egg rolls, wontons, and other savory snacks were enjoyed only by members of China's imperial household. Their royal chefs concocted the savory delicacies for special banquets.

■ Soak mushrooms for 30 minutes in enough warm water to cover. Rinse well; squeeze to drain. Finely chop, discarding stems. Soak bean threads for 15 minutes in enough warm water to cover. Drain well; squeeze out excess moisture. Cut into 2-inch lengths. Thaw shrimp, if frozen. Finely chop shrimp and pork. For sauce, mix water, oyster sauce, wine, and cornstarch.

■ Pour 1 tablespoon oil into a large skillet. (Add more oil as needed during cooking.) Preheat over medium-high heat. Stir-fry gingerroot and garlic in hot oil for 15 seconds. Add carrot, sprouts, and onions; stir-fry for 1 to 1½ minutes or till crisp-tender. Remove. Add shrimp; stir-fry for 1 to 2 minutes or till pink. Remove. Add pork; stir-fry for 2 to 3 minutes or till no pink remains. Push meat from center. Stir sauce. Add to center. Cook and stir till bubbly. Cook and stir 1 minute more. Return shrimp and vegetables. Add bean threads and mushrooms. Stir to coat with sauce. Remove and cool.

■ In a wok or 3-quart saucepan heat 1½ to 2 inches cooking oil to 365°. Fill wrappers as directed on page 94 or 98. Fry, a few at a time, in hot oil for 1 to 2½ minutes or till golden, turning once. Remove from oil. Drain on paper towels. Keep warm in a 300° oven while frying remaining food. Serve warm with Sweet-and-Sour Dipping Sauce, Honey Dipping Sauce, or Chinese Mustard Sauce. Makes 16 appetizer servings.

Nutrition information per serving: 164 calories, 7 g protein, 16 g carbohydrate, 8 g fat (1 g saturated), 30 mg cholesterol, 286 mg sodium, 174 mg potassium.

TEMPURA

JAPANESE
SPECIALTY

Spanish and Portugese missionaries to Japan developed tempura because it reminded them of foods from home. The Japanese have extended the concept to include many types of fish, shellfish, and vegetables.

8 *ounces fresh* or *frozen peeled and deveined medium shrimp*
8 *ounces fresh* or *frozen fish fillets (about ¼ inch thick)*
Cooking oil or *shortening for deep-fat frying*
Sherry Dipping Sauce (see recipe, below) and/or *Chili Dipping Sauce, Sweet-and-Sour Dipping Sauce, Spicy Dipping Sauce, Chinese Mustard Sauce, Honey Dipping Sauce,* or *Vinegar Dipping Sauce (see recipes, pages 112 and 113) (optional)*

2 *cups all-purpose flour*
½ *teaspoon baking soda*
¼ *teaspoon salt*
2 *beaten egg yolks*
2 *cups ice water*
3 *cups mixed fresh vegetables (asparagus, cut into 2-inch pieces; broccoli flowerets; sweet potato slices; mushroom halves; sweet peppers, cut into thin strips; and/or carrots, cut into thin strips)*

■ Thaw shrimp and fish, if frozen. Cut fish into bite-size pieces. In a wok or 3-quart saucepan heat 1½ to 2 inches of cooking oil or shortening to 365°. If desired, prepare one or more of the dipping sauces. Meanwhile, for batter, in a mixing bowl combine flour, baking soda, and salt. Make a well in the center of the dry ingredients. Combine egg yolks and ice water; add all at once to flour mixture. Stir just till combined (a few lumps should remain).

■ Dip shrimp, fish pieces, and vegetables into batter, a few pieces at a time, swirling to coat. Fry, a few pieces at a time, in the hot oil for 2 to 3 minutes or till golden, turning once. Using a wire strainer or slotted spoon, remove food from oil. Drain on a wok rack or on paper towels. Keep warm in a 300° oven while frying remaining pieces. Serve warm. If desired, serve with dipping sauces. Makes 10 appetizer servings.

SHERRY DIPPING SAUCE: In a saucepan combine 1 cup *chicken broth,* 2 tablespoons *soy sauce,* 2 tablespoons *dry sherry,* and 1 tablespoon *white vinegar.* Heat mixture just to boiling. Serve warm.

Nutrition information per serving with Sherry Dipping Sauce: 309 calories, 12 g protein, 23 g carbohydrate, 18 g fat (3 g saturated), 85 mg cholesterol, 435 mg sodium, 241 mg potassium.

FRIED CURRIED TURNOVERS

1 15-ounce package folded
    refrigerated unbaked pie-
    crusts (2 crusts)
1 large boneless, skinless
    chicken breast half
    (4 ounces)
1 tablespoon cooking oil
2 cloves garlic, minced
1 medium carrot, shredded
    (½ cup)

1 small onion, finely chopped
    (⅓ cup)
4 ounces lean ground beef
    or pork
2 to 3 teaspoons curry powder
¼ teaspoon salt
⅛ teaspoon pepper
    Cooking oil or shortening
    for deep-fat frying

**VIETNAMESE
SPECIALTY**
*The cuisines of
Vietnam, China, and
the Philippines all
include meat-filled fried
pastries. We've made
this typical Vietnamese
pastry simpler by
starting with refriger-
ated piecrust.*

■ Let piecrusts stand at room temperature for 20 minutes. Unfold crusts. Cut into 16 to 18 four-inch circles, rerolling as necessary. Set aside.

■ Rinse chicken and pat dry. Finely chop. Set aside.

■ For filling, pour the 1 tablespoon cooking oil into a large skillet. (Add more oil as necessary during cooking.) Preheat over medium-high heat. Stir-fry garlic in hot oil for 15 seconds. Add carrot and onion. Stir-fry for 2 minutes. Remove from the skillet. Add the chicken and beef or pork. Stir-fry for 2 to 3 minutes or till no pink remains. Drain. Add curry powder; stir-fry 1 minute more. Return vegetables to the skillet. Stir in salt and pepper. Remove all ingredients from skillet and cool.

■ In a wok or 3-quart saucepan heat 1½ to 2 inches of cooking oil or shortening to 365°. Meanwhile place about *2 tablespoons* of the filling in the center of *each* pastry circle. Fold the pastry over the filling, making half circles. Moisten the edges with water. Pinch to seal. Fry pastries, a few at a time, in hot oil for 3 to 5 minutes or till golden brown, turning once.

■ Using a wire strainer or slotted spoon, remove pastries from the oil. Drain on a wok rack or on paper towels. Keep warm in a 300° oven while frying remaining pastries. Serve warm. Makes 16 to 18 appetizer servings.

Nutrition information per serving: 170 calories, 4 g protein, 13 g carbohydrate, 11 g fat (8 g saturated), 10 mg cholesterol, 147 mg sodium, 66 mg potassium.

Cantonese Lemon Chicken

CANTONESE LEMON CHICKEN

4 medium boneless, skinless
    chicken breast halves
    (12 ounces total)
    Cooking oil or shortening
    for deep-fat frying
⅓ cup all-purpose flour
¼ cup cornstarch
¼ teaspoon salt
⅓ cup water
2 tablespoons cooking oil
4 ounces rice sticks or 3 cups
    hot cooked rice

1 cup chicken broth
2 tablespoons sugar
2 tablespoons lemon juice
4 teaspoons cornstarch
3 green onions, cut into thin
    slivers
1½ cups shredded lettuce
    Lemon slices
    Carrot cutout (see directions
    for Creative Cutouts, page
    194) (optional)
    Lemon thyme (optional)
    Edible flowers (optional)

CHINESE SPECIALTY
For this popular Cantonese entreé, you deep-fry bits of chicken to a golden crispness and glaze them with a fresh, tart lemon sauce.

炒
鍋
烹
飪

■ Rinse chicken and pat dry. Cut into 1-inch pieces; set aside. In a wok or 3-quart saucepan heat 1½ to 2 inches of cooking oil or shortening to 365°.

■ For batter, combine flour, the ¼ cup cornstarch, and salt. Add the water and the 2 tablespoons cooking oil. Using a rotary beater or wire whisk, beat till smooth. (If batter is too thick, stir in 1 tablespoon of additional water.) Dip chicken into the batter, swirling to coat. Allow excess batter to drip off. Fry chicken, a few pieces at a time, in hot oil for 4 to 5 minutes or till golden brown and chicken is no longer pink, turning once. Using a wire strainer or slotted spoon, remove chicken from oil. Drain on a wok rack or on paper towels. Keep warm in a 300° oven while frying remaining chicken.

■ Meanwhile, in a large saucepan cook rice sticks (if using) in boiling water for 1 to 2 minutes or just till tender. Drain and keep warm. For sauce, in a medium saucepan combine the chicken broth, sugar, lemon juice, and the 4 teaspoons cornstarch. Cook and stir till thickened and bubbly. Cook and stir for 2 minutes more. Add the slivered onions, stirring gently to coat.

■ On 4 dinner plates arrange chicken over hot cooked rice sticks or rice and shredded lettuce. Drizzle with sauce. Garnish with lemon slices and, if desired, carrot cutout, lemon thyme, and edible flowers. Serve immediately. Makes 4 servings.

Nutrition information per serving: 537 calories, 24 g protein, 45 g carbohydrate, 28 g fat (4 g saturated), 54 mg cholesterol, 382 mg sodium, 310 mg potassium.

SWEET-AND-SOUR FISH

Sweet-and-sour sauce tastes just as good on fish as it does on the more traditional pork. Here nuggets of fish, celery, peppers, and water chestnuts mingle in the tangy, yet sweet sauce.

1¼ pounds halibut steaks, cut 1 inch thick
½ cup apple or orange juice
¼ cup packed brown sugar
¼ cup red wine vinegar
2 tablespoons hoisin sauce
4 teaspoons cornstarch
1 tablespoon soy sauce
Cooking oil or shortening for deep-fat frying
⅓ cup all-purpose flour
⅓ cup water
¼ cup cornstarch

2 tablespoons cooking oil
1 tablespoon cooking oil
2 cloves garlic, minced
1 teaspoon grated gingerroot
2 medium stalks celery, sliced (1 cup)
1 medium green pepper, cut into 1-inch pieces (1 cup)
1 medium sweet red pepper, cut into 1-inch pieces (1 cup)
1 8-ounce can sliced water chestnuts, drained
3 cups hot cooked rice

■ Cut fish into 1-inch cubes, discarding skin and bones. Set aside. For sauce, stir together apple or orange juice, brown sugar, wine vinegar, hoisin sauce, the 4 teaspoons cornstarch, and the soy sauce. Set aside.

■ In a wok or 3-quart saucepan heat 1½ to 2 inches cooking oil or shortening to 365°. Meanwhile, for batter combine flour, water, the ¼ cup cornstarch, and the 2 tablespoons cooking oil. Using a rotary beater or wire whisk, beat till smooth. Dip fish pieces into batter, swirling to coat. Fry fish, a few pieces at a time, in the hot oil for 3 to 4 minutes or till golden, turning once. Remove fish from hot oil. Drain on a wok rack or on paper towels. Keep warm in a 300° oven while frying remaining fish.

■ Pour the 1 tablespoon cooking oil into a large skillet. (Add more oil as necessary during cooking.) Preheat over medium-high heat. Stir-fry garlic and gingerroot in hot oil for 15 seconds. Add celery; stir-fry for 1 minute. Add green and red pepper; stir-fry for 2 minutes. Add water chestnuts; stir-fry 1 minute more. Push from the center of the wok. Stir sauce. Add to the center of the wok. Cook and stir till thickened and bubbly. Stir all ingredients together to coat with sauce. Cook and stir 1 minute more. Arrange fish on rice. Spoon vegetable mixture atop. Serve immediately. Serves 4.

Nutrition information per serving: 735 calories, 32 g protein, 89 g carbohydrate, 27 g fat (4 g saturated), 38 mg cholesterol, 549 mg sodium, 964 mg potassium.

SWEET-AND-SOUR PORK

12 ounces lean boneless pork
2 tablespoons mirin or dry
    sherry
2 tablespoons soy sauce
1 teaspoon sesame oil
1 cup chicken broth
⅓ cup sugar
⅓ cup red wine vinegar
4 teaspoons cornstarch
1 tablespoon soy sauce
    Cooking oil or shortening
    for deep-fat frying
1 beaten egg
½ cup cornstarch
½ cup all-purpose flour

½ cup chicken broth
1 tablespoon cooking oil
1 clove garlic, minced
3 medium carrots, thinly bias
    sliced (1½ cups)
1 medium green pepper, cut
    into 1-inch pieces (1 cup)
1 medium sweet red pepper, cut
    into 1-inch pieces (1 cup)
3 green onions, bias sliced into
    1-inch pieces (½ cup)
1 8-ounce can pineapple chunks
    (juice pack), drained
3 cups hot cooked rice

CHINESE SPECIALTY
It's an unbeatable combination—deep-fried batter-coated pork with vegetables and pineapple. The sauce that glazes them is neither sweet nor sour, but a little of both.

炒鍋烹飪

■ Trim fat from pork. Cut into ¾-inch cubes. Set aside. For marinade, stir together mirin, 2 tablespoons soy sauce, and sesame oil. Pour over pork. Toss to coat. Cover; let stand at room temperature for 20 minutes. For sauce, stir together the 1 cup broth, sugar, vinegar, 4 teaspoons cornstarch, and 1 tablespoon soy sauce. Set aside. In a wok or 3-quart saucepan heat 1½ to 2 inches of cooking oil or shortening to 365°. Meanwhile, for batter, stir together egg, the ½ cup cornstarch, flour, and the ½ cup broth till smooth.

■ Drain pork; pat dry. Dip into batter, swirling to coat. Fry, a few pieces at a time, for 4 to 5 minutes or till no pink remains. Remove from oil. Drain on paper towels. Keep warm in a 300° oven while frying remaining pork.

■ Pour the 1 tablespoon oil into a large skillet. (Add more oil as necessary during cooking.) Preheat over medium-high heat. Stir-fry garlic in hot oil for 15 seconds. Add carrots; stir-fry for 4 to 5 minutes or till crisp-tender. Remove. Add peppers and onions. Stir-fry for 1½ to 2 minutes or till crisp-tender. Remove. Stir sauce. Add to skillet. Cook and stir till bubbly. Cook and stir for 2 minutes more. Stir in pineapple and the cooked vegetables. Cook and stir about 1 minute more or till hot. Arrange pork on rice. Spoon vegetable mixture atop. Serve immediately. Makes 4 servings.

Nutrition information per serving: 804 calories, 29 g protein, 103 g carbohydrate, 30 g fat (6 g saturated), 111 mg cholesterol, 1,177 mg sodium, 765 mg potassium.

BEEF WITH CRISPY BASIL

THAI SPECIALTY
Deep-frying the basil gives it a glossy green color and adds texture to this dish. Similar beef dishes are also typical of Korea.

1 pound beef flank steak
    or top round steak
2 tablespoons fish sauce
1 tablespoon soy sauce
1 teaspoon sugar
2 cloves garlic, minced
¼ teaspoon pepper

32 fresh basil leaves
   Cooking oil or shortening
    for deep-fat frying
   Vinegar Dipping Sauce
    (see recipe, page 112)
   Carrot shreds (optional)
   Edible flowers (optional)

■ Trim any fat from beef. Partially freeze beef. Thinly slice across the grain into bite-size strips. In a bowl combine the fish sauce, soy sauce, sugar, garlic, and pepper. Add beef strips, tossing to coat. Let stand at room temperature for 30 minutes, stirring once or twice.

■ Wash the basil leaves. Pat leaves *completely dry* with paper towels. Then place leaves in a single layer on paper towels. Let stand at room temperature for 30 minutes; pat leaves dry again with paper towels.

■ Meanwhile, in a wok or 3-quart saucepan heat 1½ to 2 inches of cooking oil or shortening to 365°. Place some of the meat strips in a wire strainer or frying basket. Fry strips in hot oil for 30 to 45 seconds or just till brown. Remove from oil and drain on paper towels. Repeat with remaining beef. Keep warm in a 300° oven while frying basil.

■ *Carefully* fry the basil leaves, about *one-third* at a time, for 5 to 10 seconds or till glossy green. Using a wire strainer or slotted spoon, remove from the hot oil. Drain on paper towels. Sprinkle over beef. Sprinkle with Vinegar Dipping Sauce. If desired, garnish with carrot shreds and edible flowers. Makes 4 servings.

Nutrition information per serving: 477 calories, 25 g protein, 5 g carbohydrate, 40 g fat (9 g saturated), 60 mg cholesterol, 1,743 mg sodium, 608 mg potassium.

Beef with Crispy Basil

DEEP-FRIED PORK CUTLETS

JAPANESE SPECIALTY
Known as fast food in Tokyo, fried pork cutlets (called "Tonkatsu") are a popular meal.

1 pound boneless pork sirloin
  or *tenderloin*
⅓ cup all-purpose flour
¼ teaspoon salt
⅛ teaspoon pepper
1 beaten egg
1 tablespoon water

⅔ cup fine dry bread crumbs
  Cooking oil or *shortening*
  for deep-fat frying
2 cups finely shredded cabbage
  Vinegar Dipping Sauce
  (see recipe, page 112)

■ Trim fat from pork. Cut into 8 equal size pieces. Place each piece between 2 pieces of clear plastic wrap. Pound to ¼-inch thickness. Remove plastic wrap. Cut small slits around edges of the pork to prevent curling. In a shallow dish stir together the flour, salt, and pepper. In another shallow dish combine the egg and the water. Place bread crumbs on a piece of waxed paper or in a third shallow dish.

■ Coat each piece of pork with the flour mixture. Dip into the egg mixture. Coat with the bread crumbs. Set aside.

■ In a wok or 3-quart saucepan heat 1½ to 2 inches of cooking oil or shortening to 365°. Meanwhile, mound *one-fourth* of the shredded cabbage on *each* of 4 dinner plates; set aside.

■ Fry pork cutlets, 1 or 2 at a time, in the hot oil about 3 minutes or till golden brown and no pink remains, turning once. Using metal tongs, remove pork from the oil. Drain on a wok rack or on paper towels. Keep warm in a 300° oven while frying remaining cutlets.

■ To serve, slice each cutlet crosswise into ½-inch strips. Reassemble cutlets atop cabbage. Spoon Vinegar Dipping Sauce over the cutlets or use for dipping. Makes 4 servings.

Nutrition information per serving: 664 calories, 29 g protein, 23 g carbohydrate, 51 g fat (9 g saturated), 131 mg cholesterol, 1,109 mg sodium, 475 mg potassium.

SESAME PUFFS

2 cups all-purpose flour
1 tablespoon finely shredded
   lemon peel
1 teaspoon baking powder
¼ teaspoon salt
⅛ teaspoon ground cardamom
¼ cup margarine or butter

⅔ cup sugar
2 eggs
  Cooking oil or shortening
   for deep-fat frying
1 beaten egg white
1 tablespoon water
½ cup sesame seeds

■ In a mixing bowl stir together the flour, lemon peel, baking powder, salt, and cardamom. In a mixing bowl beat the margarine or butter with an electric mixer on medium to high speed for 30 seconds. Add sugar; beat till thoroughly combined. Add eggs; beat till fluffy. Stir in the flour mixture. Turn out onto a lightly floured surface. Knead for 10 to 12 strokes or till dough clings together. Roll dough into a log about 1½ inches in diameter.

■ In a wok or 3-quart saucepan heat 1½ to 2 inches of cooking oil or shortening to 365°. Meanwhile, cut dough into ½-inch slices. Roll each slice into a ball. Stir together the egg white and the water. Roll each ball in the egg white mixture, then in sesame seeds to coat lightly.

■ Fry balls of dough, a few at a time, in hot oil for 3 to 5 minutes or till golden brown and balls begin to expand and crack, turning once. Using a wire strainer or slotted spoon, remove balls from hot oil. Drain on a wok rack or on paper towels. Keep warm in a 300° oven while frying remaining balls. Serve warm. Makes 8 servings.

Nutrition information per serving: 427 calories, 8 g protein, 42 g carbohydrate, 26 g fat (4 g saturated), 53 mg cholesterol, 197 mg sodium, 99 mg potassium.

CHINESE SPECIALTY

As these Sesame Puffs are fried, they form large cracks that resemble laughing mouths. **(Pictured on pages 88 and 89.)**

MINIATURE FIRECRACKERS

½ of an 8-ounce package (⅔ cup)
   pitted whole dates
¼ *cup finely chopped walnuts*
1 *teaspoon finely shredded*
   orange peel

Orange juice (optional)
24 *wonton wrappers*
   Cooking oil or *shortening*
    for deep-fat frying
   Sifted powdered sugar

To make each firecracker, position a wonton wrapper with a point toward you. Spread about 1 teaspoon of the filling in a strip about 1¼ inches from the bottom point. Roll the bottom point of the wonton wrapper over the filling, tucking it under the filling. Continue rolling the wonton into a log, completely enclosing the filling.

■ Using a knife that has been dipped in water, finely chop the dates. For filling, in a medium bowl stir together the dates, walnuts, and orange peel. If filling is too dry to stick together, add 1 to 2 tablespoons orange juice.

■ For *each* firecracker, position a wonton wrapper with a point toward you. Spread *1 teaspoon* of filling across and just below the center of the wrapper. Fold the bottom point of the wonton wrapper over filling; tuck point under filling. Roll up wrapper into a log so that the filling is completely enclosed. Wet top point and press to seal. Wet the inside of each end of roll; twist and pinch ends to seal. Repeat with the remaining wrappers and filling.

■ In a wok or 3-quart saucepan heat 1½ to 2 inches cooking oil to 365°. Fry, a few at a time, in hot oil for 1 to 1½ minutes or till golden, turning once. Remove from oil. Drain on paper towels. Keep warm in a 300° oven while frying remaining pastry. Sprinkle with sugar. Makes 12 servings.

Nutrition information per serving: 93 calories, 1 g protein, 12 g carbohydrate, 5 g fat (0 g saturated), 0 mg cholesterol, 53 mg sodium, 75 mg potassium.

USING CHOPSTICKS

Try this easy-holding technique: Place one chopstick, about two-thirds of its length from the narrow tip, in the curve at the base of your thumb. Let this stick rest on the end of your ring finger. Then, close the base of your thumb over the stick to hold it firm. This stick does not move.

   Hold the second chopstick firmly between the tip of your thumb and your index finger on the same hand, with the middle finger resting on the first stick. To pick up food, move the top stick up and down. Use an open and close motion for eating.

FRIED STUFFED BANANAS

2 tablespoons finely chopped
   walnuts
1½ teaspoons sugar
¼ teaspoon finely shredded
   lemon peel
¾ cup all-purpose flour
¼ cup cornstarch
2 tablespoons sugar

1 teaspoon baking powder
⅔ cup water
1 tablespoon cooking oil
   Cooking oil or shortening
      for deep-fat frying
2 firm large bananas
   Sifted powdered sugar

**VIETNAMESE
SPECIALTY**
*Bananas are the base
for many Vietnamese
desserts because they
grow locally. Try
serving these nut-filled
bananas with ice
cream.*

炒
餉
烹
飪

■ For filling, in a small bowl stir together the walnuts, the 1½ teaspoons sugar, and the lemon peel. Set aside.

■ For batter, in a small mixing bowl combine the flour, cornstarch, the 2 tablespoons sugar, and the baking powder. In another bowl stir together the water and the 1 tablespoon cooking oil. Add all at once to the flour mixture. Using a rotary beater or wire whisk, beat till smooth.

■ In a wok or 3-quart saucepan heat 1½ to 2 inches of cooking oil or shortening to 365°.

■ Meanwhile, peel the bananas and halve crosswise. Split each half lengthwise. Slightly hollow out the center of each banana quarter. Spoon the filling into the center. Place the quarters back together, forming banana halves with filling in the center.

■ Dip the banana halves into the batter, swirling to coat. Fry banana halves, two at a time, in the hot oil about 2 minutes or till the bananas are golden brown, turning once. Using a wire strainer or slotted spoon, remove bananas from the oil. Drain on a wok rack or on paper towels. Keep warm in a 300° oven while frying remaining banana halves. Sprinkle with sifted powdered sugar. Serve warm. Makes 4 servings.

Nutrition information per serving: 408 calories, 4 g protein, 47 g carbohydrate, 24 g fat (3 g saturated), 0 mg cholesterol, 75 mg sodium, 272 mg potassium.

Sauces

Specialty sauces are as basic to Oriental kitchens as salt and pepper are to American kitchens. Whether they're served hot or cold, these sauces enhance a variety of foods and often give a recipe its special Oriental flavor.

CHILI DIPPING SAUCE

In a small bowl stir together ¼ cup *soy sauce,* 2 tablespoons *white vinegar,* and ¼ teaspoon bottled *hot pepper sauce.* Makes about ⅓ cup.

Nutrition information per tablespoon: 7 calories, 1 g protein, 1 g carbohydrate, 0 g fat, 0 mg cholesterol, 778 mg sodium, 25 mg potassium.

SWEET-AND-SOUR DIPPING SAUCE

In a small saucepan stir together ½ cup packed *brown sugar* and 1 tablespoon *cornstarch.* Stir in ⅓ cup *chicken broth;* ⅓ cup *red wine vinegar;* 1 tablespoon *soy sauce;* 1 clove *garlic,* minced; and 1 teaspoon grated *gingerroot.* Cook and stir till thickened and bubbly. Cook and stir 2 minutes more. Serve warm. Makes about ¾ cup.

Nutrition information per tablespoon: 40 calories, 0 g protein, 10 g carbohydrate, 0 g fat, 0 mg cholesterol, 113 mg sodium, 49 mg potassium.

VINEGAR DIPPING SAUCE

In a small bowl stir together 3 tablespoons *soy sauce* and 3 tablespoons *white vinegar.* Makes about ⅓ cup sauce.

Nutrition information per tablespoon: 5 calories, 1 g protein, 1 g carbohydrate, 0 g fat, 0 mg cholesterol, 582 mg sodium, 18 mg potassium.

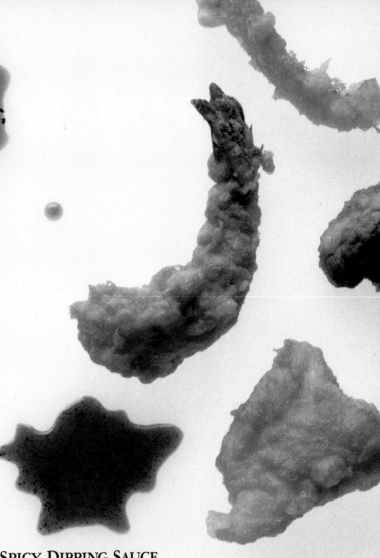

HONEY DIPPING SAUCE

In a small saucepan stir together ½ cup *honey,* 2 tablespoons *soy sauce,* 1 teaspoon grated *gingerroot,* and ¼ teaspoon *cracked black peppers.* Cook and stir till heated through. Serve warm. Makes about ⅔ cup sauce.

Nutrition information per tablespoon: 51 calories, 0 g protein, 14 g carbohydrate, 0 g fat, 0 mg cholesterol, 195 mg sodium, 19 mg potassium.

CHINESE MUSTARD SAUCE

In a small bowl stir together ¼ cup *brown mustard,* 2 tablespoons snipped *cilantro,* 2 teaspoons *water,* and 1 teaspoon *sesame oil.* Cover and refrigerate overnight. To serve, bring to room temperature. Makes about ¼ cup.

Nutrition information per tablespoon: 25 calories, 1 g protein, 2 g carbohydrate, 2 g fat (0 g saturated), 0 mg cholesterol, 195 mg sodium, 24 mg potassium.

SPICY DIPPING SAUCE

In a small saucepan stir together ⅓ cup *water,* 2 tablespoons *hoisin sauce,* 2 tablespoons *soy sauce,* 2 tablespoons *sake* or *dry sherry,* ½ teaspoon *sugar,* and ½ teaspoon *chili powder.* Heat to boiling. Reduce heat; simmer, uncovered, about 5 minutes or till reduced to ½ cup. Serve warm or cool. Makes ½ cup.

Nutrition information per tablespoon: 17 calories, 1 g protein, 3 g carbohydrate, 0 g fat, 0 mg cholesterol, 350 mg sodium, 23 mg potassium.

Simmering

Cooks of all cultures commonly use the slow, moist cooking process known as simmering. Turn the page and uncover an assortment of bubbly hot soups, including Sizzling Rice Soup, plus an array of mouth-watering main dishes, such as Japanese Simmered Pork Roast and Chinese Onion Chicken.

Gingered Chinese-Noodle Soup
(see recipe, page 120)

Simmering is one of the most common and easiest cooking techniques around. Favorite soups, stews, and meat dishes are the types of meals that simmer to perfection. Read the tips in "The Simmering Workshop," and discover just how simple simmering is.

THE SIMMERING WORKSHOP

The slow, moist cooking process commonly used for making soups, stews, pot roasts, and one-dish meals is simmering. The long cooking time allowed by simmering mellows the flavors in soups and makes larger or tougher cuts of meat more tender.

Simmering also gives you some flexibility in meal planning. Since most foods simmer for quite awhile and require very little attention, you can focus your time and attention on preparing the rest of your meal.

EQUIPMENT FOR SIMMERING

■Choose a heavy wok or large skillet with a tight-fitting lid. The thick base of a heavy wok or skillet allows even heating over a long period of time.

If you are using a steel wok, be sure the wok and the lid are well-seasoned (see page 9). If the steel is not treated, tomatoes, lemon juice, wine, vinegar, and other acidic ingredients may react with the steel and cause discoloration of the food and the wok. Although the discoloration doesn't affect the taste or safety of the food, it usually looks unappetizing.

■ When a lid is needed, make sure it is tight-fitting so moisture and steam do not escape from the wok or skillet.

GUIDES TO GOOD SIMMERING

1. Vegetables sometimes are stir-fried and meats sometimes are browned before simmering begins. To avoid a greasy finished product, be sure to drain off all excess fat before adding the simmering liquid.

2. When the liquid is added, you will need to bring the soup or meat mixture to boiling. Then, reduce the heat slightly so the bubbles slowly rise toward the surface, breaking just before they reach the top.

3. Sometimes the wok or skillet will need to be covered to keep all of the liquid and steam inside. Other times, however, the wok or skillet should be uncovered to reduce the mixture's quantity or to thicken the mixture slightly.

4. In some recipes a mixture of flour or cornstarch and liquid is added to the cooking liquid. Make sure you add the flour or cornstarch mixture at the time directed in the recipe. If it's added too soon, the flavorful sauce or gravy will tend to thin after it thickens.

CORN AND CHICKEN SOUP

2 medium boneless, skinless
    chicken breast halves
    (6 ounces total)
¼ cup water
1 tablespoon rice wine or dry
    white wine

2 teaspoons soy sauce
1 teaspoon grated gingerroot
1 teaspoon sesame oil
2½ cups chicken broth
1 cup loose-pack frozen corn
1 beaten egg

■ Rinse chicken and pat dry. Finely chop chicken. In a bowl stir together the chicken, water, rice wine or dry white wine, soy sauce, gingerroot, and sesame oil. Cover and let stand at room temperature for 20 minutes.

■ In a wok or 3-quart saucepan combine the chicken broth and corn; bring to boiling. Add the chicken mixture, stirring constantly to separate chicken pieces. Return to boiling. Reduce heat and simmer, uncovered, about 2 minutes or till no pink remains in chicken, stirring often.

■ Pour the beaten egg into the hot chicken mixture in a steady stream while stirring 2 or 3 times to create shreds. Remove from heat. Cover and let stand for 1 minute. Ladle into soup bowls. Makes 6 side-dish servings.

Nutrition information per serving: 98 calories, 11 g protein, 7 g carbohydrate, 3 g fat (1 g saturated), 54 mg cholesterol, 466 mg sodium, 200 mg potassium.

CHINESE SPECIALTY
Use the Chinese trick of pouring egg into soup while stirring a few times to form thin, lacy shreds. The shreds will float to the top, making an attractive self-garnish.

炒
锅
烹
饪

SIZZLING RICE SOUP

Speed is of the essence when making Sizzling Rice Soup. If you don't work quickly when pouring the chicken broth mixture over the hot rice patties, you'll lose the sizzle.

2 cups cooked rice
  Cooking oil or shortening
    for deep-fat frying
½ of a 6-ounce package frozen
    pea pods (1 cup)
5 cups chicken broth

1 medium carrot, cut into
    carrot flowers (see
    directions, page 64) or
    thinly sliced (½ cup)
1 green onion, sliced
    (2 tablespoons)
1 cup chopped cooked chicken
½ cup chopped bok choy
    or cabbage

■ Spread the rice evenly in a greased 8x4x2-inch loaf pan. Unmold the rice onto a greased baking sheet. Bake, uncovered, in a 300° oven for 1½ to 2 hours or till dry, turning once. Cool and break into eight 2-inch pieces. In a 3-quart saucepan heat 1½ to 2 inches cooking oil or shortening to 365°. Fry the dried rice patties, a few at a time, in the hot oil for 40 to 60 seconds or till light brown and crisp. Using a wire strainer or slotted spoon, remove from oil. Drain on paper towels. Keep the rice patties warm in a 300° oven while preparing the soup.

■ For soup, run pea pods under cold water till they can be broken apart. Cut diagonally into 1-inch lengths. In a wok combine the chicken broth, carrot, and green onion. Bring to boiling. Reduce heat. Simmer, uncovered, for 3 minutes. Add pea pods, chicken, and bok choy or cabbage. Simmer, uncovered, for 2 minutes more. Keep warm.

■ Working quickly, place all of the hot rice patties in a serving bowl. Pour chicken broth mixture atop rice patties. Makes 8 side-dish servings.

Nutrition information per serving: 191 calories, 10 g protein, 17 g carbohydrate, 9 g fat (1 g saturated), 15 mg cholesterol, 503 mg sodium, 262 mg potassium.

Sizzling Rice Soup

GINGERED CHINESE-NOODLE SOUP

CHINESE SPECIALTY
*Noodles symbolize longevity in the Chinese culture, making them a traditional birthday food. **Gingered Chinese-Noodle Soup** is not only festive enough for birthdays, but is appropriate for other holidays, too. (**Pictured on pages 114 and 115.**)*

1 tablespoon cooking oil
2 cloves garlic, minced
1 teaspoon grated gingerroot
1 medium sweet red or green pepper, cut into thin strips (1 cup)
1 medium carrot, thinly sliced (½ cup)
1 small onion, finely chopped (⅓ cup)
4 cups chicken broth

1 tablespoon soy sauce
⅛ teaspoon crushed red pepper
3 ounces steamed or fresh Chinese egg noodles, 2 ounces dried Chinese egg noodles, or 2 ounces fine egg noodles
1 cup thinly sliced fresh mushrooms
1 cup fresh pea pods, halved
1 tablespoon lemon juice

■ Pour cooking oil into a wok or large skillet. Preheat over medium-high heat. Stir-fry garlic and gingerroot in hot oil for 15 seconds. Add red or green pepper, carrot, and onion. Stir-fry for 2 minutes. Add chicken broth, soy sauce, and red pepper. Bring to boiling. Reduce heat. Simmer, covered, for 2 minutes. Stir in noodles and mushrooms. Return to boiling. Reduce heat. Simmer, covered, for 4 to 6 minutes or till noodles and mushrooms are tender. Stir in pea pods. Simmer, uncovered, for 1 to 2 minutes or till pea pods are crisp-tender. Stir in lemon juice. Makes 6 side-dish servings.

Nutrition information per serving: 114 calories, 6 g protein, 14 g carbohydrate, 4 g fat (1 g saturated), 16 mg cholesterol, 700 mg sodium, 358 mg potassium.

KEEPING GINGER FRESH

Chinese cooks use gingerroot almost every day. But if you plan on using it only occasionally, these storage hints will be helpful.

For short-term storage, wrap the root in a paper towel and refrigerate it for up to 3 weeks. For storage up to 3 months, immerse peeled slices of gingerroot in dry sherry or cooking oil and refrigerate them. Or, for storage up to 1 year, wrap the gingerroot in moisture- and vapor-proof wrap and freeze. Grate or cut off amounts of the frozen gingerroot as needed.

HOT-AND-SOUR SOUP

8 ounces lean boneless pork
1 teaspoon cornstarch
1 teaspoon soy sauce
1 teaspoon rice wine or dry
    white wine
½ teaspoon sesame oil
4 dried wood ears
4 dried mushrooms
2 14½-ounce cans (3½ cups)
    chicken broth

¼ cup rice vinegar or white
    vinegar
2 tablespoons soy sauce
1 teaspoon sugar
1 teaspoon grated gingerroot
½ teaspoon pepper
1 tablespoon cold water
2 teaspoons cornstarch
1 beaten egg
1 green onion, thinly sliced
    (2 tablespoons)

CHINESE SPECIALTY
Delightfully peppery and vinegary, this soup has warmed north and central China for centuries.

■ Trim fat from pork. Partially freeze pork. Thinly slice across the grain into bite-size strips. Stack strips and cut into shreds. Stir together the 1 teaspoon cornstarch, 1 teaspoon soy sauce, rice wine, and sesame oil. Toss with the pork. Let stand at room temperature for 30 minutes.

■ Meanwhile, soak wood ears and mushrooms for 30 minutes in enough warm water to cover. Rinse well and squeeze to drain thoroughly. Slice thinly, discarding stems.

■ In a wok or 3-quart saucepan combine the chicken broth, vinegar, the 2 tablespoons soy sauce, sugar, gingerroot, and pepper. Bring to boiling. Stir in pork, wood ears, and mushrooms. Return to boiling. Reduce heat. Simmer, covered, for 2 to 3 minutes or till no pink remains in pork.

■ Stir together cold water and the 2 teaspoons cornstarch. Stir into the chicken broth mixture. Cook and stir till slightly thickened and bubbly. Cook and stir for 2 minutes more. Pour the egg into the soup in a steady stream while stirring 2 or 3 times to create shreds. Remove from heat. Stir in green onion. Makes 6 side-dish servings.

Nutrition information per serving: 134 calories, 13 g protein, 7 g carbohydrate, 6 g fat (2 g saturated), 62 mg cholesterol, 884 mg sodium, 341 mg potassium.

SPRING ROLLS

VIETNAMESE SPECIALTY
Spring rolls are the Vietnamese version of Chinese egg rolls. Instead of a dough wrapper, they are made with translucent rice paper.

1¾ *cups chicken broth*
¾ *cup white vinegar*
½ *teaspoon pepper*
2 *large boneless, skinless chicken breast halves (8 ounces total)*
1 *medium red onion, sliced and separated into rings (¾ cup)*
12 *fresh* or *frozen peeled and deveined small shrimp*

½ *ounce rice sticks*
12 *8-inch round rice papers*
   Lettuce leaves
1 *small cucumber, sliced and cut into strips (1 cup)*
3 *tablespoons snipped mint leaves*
12 *sprigs cilantro* or *parsley Nuoc Cham Sauce*

■ In a wok combine the chicken broth, vinegar, and pepper. Bring to boiling. Rinse chicken. Add chicken and onion to the wok. Simmer, covered, for 15 to 20 minutes or till no pink remains in chicken. Remove chicken. Add fresh or frozen shrimp. Boil for 1 to 3 minutes or till shrimp turn pink. Drain. Chill the chicken, shrimp, and onion. Soak the rice sticks for 15 minutes in enough warm water to cover. Drain well. Squeeze out excess moisture. Cut into 1-inch lengths. Thinly slice the chicken. Halve the shrimp lengthwise. Set aside.

■ Carefully dip each rice paper quickly in water and place between damp cotton dish towels. Let stand 10 minutes. To assemble, remove 1 rice paper from between towels. Place some lettuce, cucumber strips, mint, cilantro or parsley sprigs, chicken slices, onion rings, and rice sticks on rice paper about 1 inch from the edge. Roll up tightly, just far enough to enclose filling. Place 2 shrimp halves on the rice paper next to the filling. Fold 2 sides of rice paper over filling and shrimp. Continue rolling up. Repeat with remaining ingredients. Serve with Nuoc Cham Sauce. Makes 12 appetizer servings.

NUOC CHAM SAUCE: Combine 3 tablespoons *water;* 1 tablespoon *fish sauce;* 1 tablespoon *lime juice;* 2 teaspoons *sugar;* 1 teaspoon *vinegar;* 1 clove *garlic,* minced; and ⅛ teaspoon *chili paste.*

Nutrition information per serving: 94 calories, 9 g protein, 12 g carbohydrate, 1 g fat (0 g saturated), 35 mg cholesterol, 258 mg sodium, 204 mg potassium.

Quickly dip each rice paper into water and then place it between 2 clean damp cotton dish towels. Leave the rice papers between the damp towels until you use them. The moisture makes the crisp rice paper soft and flexible.

Roll up the rice paper just till the filling is enclosed. Then place 2 shrimp halves, cut side up and back to back, on the rice paper next to the filling. Fold the sides over the filling and shrimp and continue rolling, forming a packet. Only 1 layer of rice paper covers the shrimp, allowing you to see their outline through the wrapper.

ROLLED GINGER-CHICKEN SALAD

For easy summer entertaining, cook the chicken rolls and clean the vegetables a day ahead of your party. If you like, cut the peppers with a crinkle cutter to give the salad a special appearance.

4 large boneless, skinless
  chicken breast halves
  (1 pound total)
½ cup soy sauce
⅓ cup mirin or dry sherry
1 teaspoon grated gingerroot
½ cup water
2 tablespoons rice vinegar
  or white vinegar
2 tablespoons chicken broth
  or water
2 tablespoons honey
1 tablespoon cooking oil
½ teaspoon soy sauce

½ teaspoon grated gingerroot
4 cups shredded spinach
  or Chinese cabbage
1 cup fresh or half of one
  6-ounce package frozen
  pea pods, thawed
1 medium sweet red and/or
  green pepper, cut into thin
  strips (1 cup)
1 cup sliced fresh mushrooms
  Sweet red and/or green
  pepper stars (see directions
  for Creative Cutouts, page
  194) (optional)

■ Rinse chicken and pat dry. Place a chicken breast half between 2 pieces of clear plastic wrap. Working from the center to the edges, pound lightly with a meat mallet to form a rectangle about ¼ inch thick. Repeat with the remaining chicken breast halves. Place chicken in a shallow dish. In a small bowl stir together the ½ cup soy sauce, mirin or dry sherry, and 1 teaspoon gingerroot. Pour over chicken. Cover. Let stand at room temperature for 30 minutes, turning once.

■ Drain chicken, discarding marinade. Starting from a short side, roll up each chicken rectangle, jelly-roll style. Secure with string or wooden toothpicks. Place the chicken rolls and water in a wok or 3-quart saucepan. Bring to boiling; reduce heat. Simmer, covered, about 20 minutes or till no pink remains. Remove chicken rolls. Cover and chill at least 3 hours.

■ For dressing, stir together the rice vinegar or white vinegar, chicken broth or water, honey, cooking oil, the ½ teaspoon soy sauce, and the ½ teaspoon gingerroot. Cut each chicken roll into ½-inch-thick slices. On 4 individual plates, arrange spinach or cabbage, pea pods, red and/or green pepper strips, mushrooms, and chicken slices. Drizzle with dressing. If desired, garnish with pepper stars. Makes 4 servings.

Nutrition information per serving: 294 calories, 32 g protein, 20 g carbohydrate, 8 g fat (2 g saturated), 72 mg cholesterol, 2,240 mg sodium, 810 mg potassium.

Rolled Ginger-Chicken Salad

RED-COOKED CHICKEN

2 cups water
½ cup soy sauce
¼ cup rice wine **or** *dry white wine*
2 tablespoons sugar
6 1x½-inch pieces purchased dried tangerine peel **or** *Dried Tangerine Peel* (see recipe, page 82)

1 inch stick cinnamon, broken up
¼ teaspoon fennel seed, crushed
2 whole large chicken breasts, skinned and halved lengthwise, **or** 4 chicken thighs, skinned (2 pounds total)
2 green onions, sliced (¼ cup)
3 cups hot cooked rice

■ In a wok or 3-quart saucepan stir together the water, soy sauce, rice wine or dry white wine, sugar, tangerine peel, cinnamon, and fennel seed. Bring mixture to boiling. Add chicken. Return to boiling. Reduce heat. Simmer, covered, for 30 to 35 minutes or till no pink remains in chicken.

■ Remove chicken from wok, reserving cooking liquid. Cover and refrigerate the chicken. Separately chill the cooking liquid.

■ Remove the chicken meat from the bones. Cut the chicken into bite-size pieces. Remove any fat from the cooking liquid. Then, strain the liquid through a double thickness of 100 percent cotton cheesecloth. Stir in the green onions. If desired, heat the chicken in the cooking liquid. Or, in a small saucepan heat just the cooking liquid. Serve the warm or cold chicken and hot cooking liquid with hot cooked rice. Makes 4 servings.

Nutrition information per serving: 402 calories, 33 g protein, 54 g carbohydrate, 4 g fat (1 g saturated), 72 mg cholesterol, 2,129 mg sodium, 370 mg potassium.

CHINESE ONION CHICKEN

1 tablespoon cooking oil
1 tablespoon grated gingerroot
2 whole large chicken breasts, halved lengthwise (2 pounds total)
⅔ cup water
¼ cup soy sauce

2 tablespoons brown sugar
2 tablespoons cream sherry
¼ teaspoon aniseed, crushed
2 medium onions, sliced and separated into rings (1½ cups)

CHINESE SPECIALTY
Chinese cooks usually use a whole duck for this recipe. We used chicken breasts to reduce the cooking time and simplify the preparation.

炒鍋烹飪

■ Pour cooking oil into a wok or large skillet. Preheat over medium-high heat. Stir-fry gingerroot in hot oil for 15 seconds. Add chicken breasts. Quickly brown on all sides. Add the water, soy sauce, brown sugar, sherry, and aniseed. Bring to boiling. Reduce heat. Simmer, covered, for 20 to 25 minutes or till no pink remains in chicken, turning once.

■ Transfer chicken to a serving platter. Cover with foil to keep warm. Add onions to the mixture in the wok. Return to boiling. Reduce heat. Simmer, uncovered, about 15 minutes or till onions are translucent. Spoon onion mixture over the chicken breasts. Makes 4 servings.

Nutrition information per serving: 244 calories, 28 g protein, 14 g carbohydrate, 7 g fat (2 g saturated), 72 mg cholesterol, 1,100 mg sodium, 371 mg potassium.

WATCHING SODIUM CONTENT

If you're concerned about your sodium intake, it may pay you to use sodium-reduced versions of products like soy sauce and broth. As you shop, compare the sodium content of products by checking the "Nutrition information per serving" on the labels. For instance, sodium-reduced soy sauces often contain about 60 percent less sodium than their regular versions. The two products don't vary much in flavor, but you may think the sodium-reduced products make a recipe's flavor a little fuller. That's because there's less salt to mask other seasonings.

JAPANESE SPECIALTY

Japanese Simmered Pork Roast is an example of "nimono" cooking, which means the foods are simmered in seasoned liquid.

JAPANESE SIMMERED PORK ROAST

1 3-pound pork shoulder roast	¾ cup sake or dry white wine
1 tablespoon cooking oil	⅓ cup soy sauce
1¾ cups water	3 tablespoons grated gingerroot
6 green onions, cut into 1-inch lengths (about 1 cup)	4½ cups hot cooked rice (optional)

■ Trim excess fat from pork. Pour cooking oil into a wok or large skillet. Preheat over medium-high heat. Quickly brown the meat on all sides in the hot oil. Add the water, green onions, sake or wine, soy sauce, and gingerroot. Bring to boiling. Reduce heat. Simmer, covered, about 2¼ hours or till the meat is tender. Strain the juices and skim off fat. Serve juices with sliced meat. If desired, serve with hot cooked rice. Makes 6 servings.

Nutrition information per serving: 379 calories, 43 g protein, 5 g carbohydrate, 18 g fat (6 g saturated), 145 mg cholesterol, 1,040 mg sodium, 668 mg potassium.

WHAT'S A FIREPOT?

A firepot is a specialty pot used by the Chinese in much the same way as we use a fondue pot. However, instead of cooking in oil, the foods in firepots cook in simmering broth.

Firepots come in a variety of styles. The traditional shape consists of a large funnel, filled with charcoal, that is attached to a round tubular pan that holds the simmering broth mixture. Others are shaped like chafing dishes with a small stand underneath for canned heat or an alcohol lamp.

To use a traditional firepot, line a separate heatproof pan with heavy foil about 30 minutes before serving. Outdoors, pile briquettes into a pyramid on the foil-lined pan, then light. Always light the coals and use your firepot outside, because the coals produce toxic gases as they burn.

When the coals are hot, fill the firepot's round tubular pan with hot broth and then lower the coals into the firepot's center funnel. Add more coals every 20 to 30 minutes or as needed.

MONGOLIAN BEEF HOT POT

 2 ounces bean threads
1½ pounds boneless beef sirloin
      steak
 2 tablespoons soy sauce
 1 tablespoon rice wine or dry
      white wine
 1 tablespoon water
 1 teaspoon sesame oil
 8 ounces fresh or frozen peeled
      and deveined large shrimp

½ of a medium head Chinese
      cabbage, sliced about ½
      inch thick
 1 cup whole fresh mushrooms
 4 ounces tofu, cubed
 8 cups chicken broth
 4 green onions, thinly sliced
      (½ cup)
 1 tablespoon grated gingerroot

■ In a mixing bowl soak the bean threads for 15 minutes in enough warm water to cover. Drain well. Squeeze out excess moisture. Cut bean threads into 3-inch lengths. Set aside.

■ Trim fat from beef. Partially freeze beef. Thinly slice across the grain into bite-size strips. Stir together the soy sauce, rice wine or white wine, water, and sesame oil. Toss with the beef. Thaw shrimp, if frozen. Arrange beef, shrimp, cabbage, tofu, and mushrooms on a serving platter.

■ About 15 minutes before serving, in a large saucepan combine the chicken broth, green onions, and gingerroot. Bring to boiling. Pour the broth mixture into an electric wok, fondue pot, or electric skillet till the appliance is *half* full. Keep the remaining broth mixture warm and replenish the wok as necessary.

■ To serve, give each person chopsticks or a fondue fork. Have each person dip beef, shrimp, vegetables, and tofu into broth and cook to desired doneness. (Allow 1 to 2 minutes for beef, 2 to 3 minutes for shrimp, 30 seconds for cabbage, 1 to 2 minutes for mushrooms, and 1 to 2 minutes for tofu.)

■ After beef, shrimp, vegetables, and tofu have been cooked, stir bean threads into remaining broth. Ladle into soup bowls. Makes 6 servings.

Nutrition information per serving: 364 calories, 37 g protein, 11 g carbohydrate, 18 g fat (7 g saturated), 116 mg cholesterol, 1,497 mg sodium, 906 mg potassium.

CHINESE SPECIALTY

Mongolians originally introduced the hot pot or firepot to the people of China. It soon became popular all over China with resulting regional variations.

Instead of making this recipe in a firepot, you can use an electric wok, fondue pot, or electric skillet. But if you want to use a firepot, just follow the instructions in the tip box on page 128.

Steaming

Steaming has been used by cooks of the Orient for centuries. Now it's becoming increasingly popular with American cooks. In this chapter, you'll discover a sprinkling of healthful main dishes and a sampling of tasty filled buns and dumplings.

Four-Color Dumplings
(see recipe, page 143)

THE STEAMING WORKSHOP

Steaming is a simple way to cook fast and keep foods healthful at the same time. Using hot steam to cook foods helps retain all their vitamins and minerals, without adding extra fat.

With a wok, a steamer rack, and a dome-shape lid, you'll have success in making fresh-tasting, steamed foods every time.

EQUIPMENT FOR STEAMING

■A wok, with its sloping sides, is a perfect pan for steaming. Since the sides are sloped, the rack fits about halfway down inside, leaving enough room for the water below.

If you don't have a wok, you can improvise with a Dutch oven. Place three or four inverted custard cups in the bottom of a Dutch oven. Then place any kind of steamer rack on top.

■Steamer racks are available in a variety of styles. The ones typically packaged with woks are round wire racks. If your wok didn't come with a steamer rack, you may purchase one separately. Racks are available in perforated metal, bamboo, and aluminum.

The bamboo and aluminum racks can be used alone or stacked to cook more than one batch of food at a time. If they're stacked, use the steamer lid in place of the lid from the wok.

If you don't have a steamer rack you probably can make do with something you already have in your kitchen. For instance, a round wire cooling rack or a small metal colander make great replacements.

■A tight-fitting, dome-shape lid is essential for steaming. If the wok lid doesn't fit tightly, look through your regular cookware for a lid that may fit your wok. A lid from a 10- or 12-inch skillet or a Dutch oven may fit just inside the rim of the wok.

The dome shape is important because it allows condensation to run down the sides of the lid, rather than dripping on the food you are steaming.

GUIDES TO GOOD STEAMING

1. It is important to have the proper amount of water in your wok or Dutch oven. If there's too much water, it may splatter and soak the food during steaming. However, if there's too little water, the wok may boil dry during the steaming process.

When you add the water to the wok, make sure to leave 1 inch between the bottom of the steamer rack and the water. Verify the water level by placing the steamer rack in the wok, as shown in the upper left photo on page 133. After you have the water level set, bring the water to boiling over high heat.

2. When using a wire steamer rack, make sure the wires are close enough together so the food does not slip through the openings. If the food is too small, try covering the steamer rack with aluminum foil and then punching small holes through it. Or, use a round wire cooling rack instead of a steamer rack.

3. Once the water is boiling, arrange the food on the steamer rack as directed in the recipe.

4. When a recipe requires a dish in addition to the steamer rack, choose one that is heatproof and is at least 1 inch smaller than the diameter of your steamer rack.

If the dish covers all of the openings, place three or four metal jar lids on top of the steamer rack. Then place your dish atop the jar lids, as shown in the upper right photo. This will help prop the dish up enough so the steam can flow underneath and circulate freely around the dish.

5. Sometimes recipes call for foods to be covered with foil. The foil protects the food from any steam that may condense and drip on the food during steaming.

6. When you place the lid on the wok, make sure it fits tightly so very little steam escapes. Check the fit of the lid before you start. If the food you are going to cook is too large for the lid to fit snugly, look for another lid with a better fit. Make sure the lid has a dome shape so the water doesn't condense and drip on the food.

7. Check the water under the steamer rack occasionally during steaming to make sure it hasn't boiled away. Add more boiling water as necessary.

8. Any time you remove the lid from a steaming wok, do so carefully. To avoid burning yourself, be sure to tilt the lid so the steam rises away from you.

STEAMED RED CURRY CHICKEN

THAI SPECIALTY
From main dishes to desserts, coconut milk is a common ingredient in Thai cooking. The milk's natural sweetness helps balance the many hot flavors common in Thai foods.

If you have trouble finding coconut milk, a mixture of ⅔ cup light cream and ½ teaspoon coconut extract makes a good substitute in **Steamed Red Curry Chicken.**

2 large boneless, skinless chicken breast halves (8 ounces total)
1 tablespoon cooking oil
1 large fresh chili pepper, seeded (see tip, page 27)
2 slightly beaten eggs
⅔ cup canned unsweetened coconut milk

⅓ cup bamboo shoots cut into thin strips
1 small carrot, shredded (¼ cup)
1 tablespoon cornstarch
1 tablespoon fish sauce
1 teaspoon red curry paste
¼ teaspoon dried basil, crushed
3 cups hot cooked rice

■ Rinse chicken and pat dry. Cut into 1-inch pieces. Pour the cooking oil into a wok or large skillet. Preheat over medium-high heat. Add the chicken to the wok. Stir-fry for 2 to 3 minutes or till no pink remains. Remove chicken from the wok; set aside.

■ Cut the pepper into 4 thin strips and set aside. In a medium mixing bowl stir together the eggs and coconut milk. Stir in the chicken, bamboo shoots, carrot, cornstarch, fish sauce, red curry paste, and basil. Spoon chicken mixture into 4 greased 6-ounce custard cups. Top each with a pepper strip. Cover each custard cup tightly with foil.

■ Use paper towels to wipe out the wok. In the wok place a steamer rack over water. Bring water to boiling over high heat. Place custard cups on the rack. Cover and steam for 20 to 25 minutes or till a knife inserted near the center comes out clean. Serve with hot cooked rice. Makes 4 servings.

Nutrition information per serving: 431 calories, 22 g protein, 48 g carbohydrate, 17 g fat (9 g saturated), 142 mg cholesterol, 381 mg sodium, 366 mg potassium.

JAPANESE SUMMER SALAD

1 pound fresh or frozen tuna
   or swordfish steaks
   (½ to ¾ inch thick)
Salt
White pepper
4 thin lemon slices
1 cup sliced fresh mushrooms
¼ cup sake or dry sherry
¼ cup water
1½ cups somen noodles or fine
   egg noodles (6 ounces)

¼ cup water
2 tablespoons soy sauce
2 tablespoons sake or dry sherry
1 teaspoon sugar
½ teaspoon grated gingerroot
¼ teaspoon instant chicken
   bouillon granules
2 green onions, thinly sliced
   (¼ cup)

■ Thaw fish, if frozen. Cut fish into 4 serving-size pieces. Arrange the pieces in a 9-inch pie plate (or another shallow heatproof dish that is at least 1 inch smaller than the steamer rack). Sprinkle fish with salt and white pepper. Place lemon slices atop fish; cover with mushrooms. Stir together the ¼ cup sake or sherry and the ¼ cup water. Drizzle over fish, lemon slices, and mushrooms.

■ In a wok place a steamer rack over water. Bring water to boiling over high heat. Place pie plate on rack. Cover and steam for 10 to 12 minutes or till fish flakes easily when tested with a fork. Remove pie plate from steamer. Cool slightly. Discard the sake mixture and lemon slices. Cover and chill the fish and mushrooms.

■ Meanwhile, cook somen noodles or fine egg noodles in a large amount of boiling salted water till tender. Drain well. Cover with ice water. Let stand till noodles are chilled. Drain well. Cover and chill noodles till serving time.

■ For dipping sauce, stir together the ¼ cup water, soy sauce, the 2 table-spoons sake or sherry, sugar, gingerroot, and chicken bouillon granules. Cover and chill dipping sauce.

■ For each serving, arrange fish, mushrooms, and some noodles on a dinner plate. Sprinkle thinly sliced green onions over the noodles. Serve dipping sauce in small bowls on the side. Makes 4 servings.

Nutrition information per serving: 353 calories, 30 g protein, 34 g carbohydrate, 7 g fat (1 g saturated), 68 mg cholesterol, 766 mg sodium, 495 mg potassium.

JAPANESE SPECIALTY
Fish, shellfish, and practically any vegetable are combined in Japanese salads. Traditionally, Japanese serve minute portions of salad just before the start of a meal or near the end of a meal.

Keeping with typical American tastes, we increased the amount of the ingredients in this salad so you can serve it as a refreshing main dish.

Steamed Snapper

STEAMED SNAPPER

2 1¼-pound fresh or frozen
   dressed red snapper or
   other fish with heads and
   tails
1 tablespoon fish sauce
1 teaspoon finely shredded
   lemon peel
1 clove garlic, minced
4 cups shredded lettuce

1 tablespoon cooking oil
2 teaspoons grated gingerroot
4 green onions, bias sliced into
   1-inch pieces (¾ cup)
2 tablespoons soy sauce
1 teaspoon sesame oil
   Cucumber Loop (see
   directions, page 198)
   (optional)

■ Thaw fish, if frozen. Rinse and pat dry with paper towels. Score fish by making 4 diagonal cuts on the top sides, slicing *almost* to the bone. Set aside. In a small bowl stir together the fish sauce, lemon peel, and garlic; set aside.

■ In a wok place a greased steamer rack over water. Bring water to boiling over high heat. Place fish on the rack so the sides do not touch. Brush the fish sauce mixture over fish. Cover and steam for 20 to 25 minutes or till fish flakes easily with a fork. Transfer fish to a serving platter; keep warm.

■ Place lettuce on steamer rack; place rack over boiling water. Cover and steam for 1 to 2 minutes or till just limp. Arrange lettuce around fish on the serving platter; keep warm.

■ For sauce, wipe out the wok with paper towels. Pour the cooking oil into the wok. Preheat the wok over medium-high heat. Stir-fry the gingerroot in hot oil for 15 seconds. Add the green onions; stir-fry about 2 minutes or till tender. Stir in the soy sauce and sesame oil.

■ To serve, spoon some of the sauce over fish. Pass remaining sauce. If desired, garnish the platter with a Cucumber Loop. Makes 4 servings.

Nutrition information per serving: 200 calories, 30 g protein, 4 g carbohydrate, 7 g fat (1 g saturated), 50 mg cholesterol, 890 mg sodium, 742 mg potassium.

VIETNAMESE SPECIALTY

A multi-layer steamer makes preparation of this recipe even easier. Instead of steaming the lettuce after steaming the fish, place it on a separate steamer rack and add the rack to the steamer stack about 2 mintues before the fish is done.

Basic Chinese Buns

CHINESE SPECIALTY

Chinese call these sweet- or savory-filled buns "dim sum." The translation of dim sum is "to touch the heart."

3¼ to 3¾ cups all-purpose flour
1 package active dry yeast
1 cup milk
2 tablespoons sugar
1 tablespoon cooking oil

½ teaspoon salt
2 egg whites
Desired filling (see recipes, pages 139 and 142)

■ In a large mixing bowl stir together *1½ cups* of the flour and the yeast. In a small saucepan heat the milk, sugar, cooking oil, and salt just till warm (120° to 130°). Add to the flour mixture. Then add the egg whites. Beat with an electric mixer on low speed for 30 seconds, scraping sides of bowl constantly. Beat on high speed for 3 minutes. Using a spoon, stir in as much of the remaining flour as you can.

■ On a lightly floured surface knead in enough of the remaining flour to make a moderately stiff dough that is smooth and elastic (6 to 8 minutes total). Shape into a ball. Place in a lightly greased bowl, turning once to grease the surface. Cover and let rise in a warm place till double (45 to 60 minutes). Punch dough down; turn out onto a lightly floured surface. Shape into 14 balls. Cover and let rest for 10 minutes.

■ Roll or pat *each* ball of dough into a 3½-inch circle. Place filling in the center of *each* dough circle. (Use a scant 2 tablespoons savory filling or 1 tablespoon sweet filling.) Bring edges of dough up around filling, stretching dough till edges just meet; pinch to seal. Cover and let buns rest for 10 minutes.

■ Meanwhile, in a wok place a greased steamer rack over water. Bring water to boiling over high heat. Place buns, seam side down, on rack so the sides do not touch. (Cover and chill buns that don't fit on the rack.) Cover wok and steam buns for 15 to 17 minutes or till they spring back when touched. Repeat with remaining buns. Makes 14 side-dish servings.

Nutrition information per serving: 134 calories, 4 g protein, 25 g carbohydrate, 2 g fat (0 g saturated), 2 mg cholesterol, 94 mg sodium, 75 mg potassium.

EASY CHINESE BUNS

1 16-ounce package hot roll mix   *Desired filling (see recipes*
                                             below and on page 142)

■ Prepare the mix according to package directions. Cover; let rest 5 minutes. Shape into 14 balls. On a lightly floured surface, roll or pat dough into 3½-inch circles. Place filling in center of *each*. (Use a scant 2 tablespoons savory filling or 1 tablespoon sweet filling.) Bring edges of dough up around filling, stretching till edges just meet; pinch to seal. Cover; let rest for 10 minutes. In a wok place a greased steamer rack over water. Bring to boiling. Place buns, seam side down, on rack so sides do not touch. Cover wok and steam buns for 10 to 15 minutes or till they spring back when touched. Makes 14 side-dish servings.

Nutrition information per serving: 135 calories, 4 g protein, 24 g carbohydrate, 3 g fat
(0 g saturated), 15 mg cholesterol, 247 mg sodium, 51 mg potassium.

This quick and easy recipe is just as good as the traditional **Basic Chinese Buns.**
   If all the buns don't fit on the rack while steaming, cover the extras and place them in the refrigerator. After cooking the first batch, steam the buns that have been refrigerated.

CURRIED CHICKEN FILLING

2 large boneless, skinless   *1 tablespoon cooking oil*
   chicken breast halves   *6 green onions, sliced (¾ cup)*
   (8 ounces total)   *1 medium carrot, shredded*
1 teaspoon cornstarch   *(½ cup)*
1 teaspoon instant chicken   *2 teaspoons curry powder*
   bouillon granules   *¼ cup raisins*

■ Rinse chicken and pat dry; finely chop. For sauce, combine cornstarch, bouillon granules, and ¼ cup *water*. Set aside. Pour oil into a wok or large skillet. (Add more oil as necessary during cooking.) Preheat over medium-high heat. Stir-fry onions and carrot 1 to 2 minutes or till tender. Remove. Add chicken to wok. Stir-fry for 2 to 3 minutes or till no pink remains. Add curry powder; stir-fry 1 minute. Push from the center. Stir sauce. Add to center of wok. Cook and stir till bubbly. Add vegetables and raisins. Stir all ingredients together. Cook and stir 1 minute more. Makes 1½ cups filling.

Nutrition information per serving: 44 calories, 4 g protein, 4 g carbohydrate, 2 g fat
(0 g saturated), 10 mg cholesterol, 76 mg sodium, 84 mg potassium.

This exotic-flavored filling of curry and chicken perfectly fills the 14 buns yielded in the **Basic Chinese Buns** *and the* **Easy Chinese Buns.**

SILVER THREAD BUNS

<table>
<tr><td>

2¾ to 3¼ cups all-purpose flour
  1 package active dry yeast
  1 cup water
  2 tablespoons sugar
  1 tablespoon margarine, butter,
       or lard
</td><td>

¼ teaspoon salt
¼ cup margarine, butter,
      or lard, softened
2 tablespoons sugar
      Black sesame seed (optional)
</td></tr>
</table>

■ In a large mixing bowl stir together *1¼ cups* of the flour and the yeast. Heat and stir the water, 2 tablespoons sugar, the 1 tablespoon margarine, and the salt just till warm (120° to 130°) and margarine almost melts. Add to the flour mixture.

■ Beat with an electric mixer on low speed for 30 seconds, scraping the sides of the bowl constantly. Beat on high speed for 3 minutes. Using a spoon, stir in as much of the remaining flour as you can. On a lightly floured surface, knead in enough of the remaining flour to make a moderately stiff dough that is smooth and elastic (6 to 8 minutes total). Shape dough into a ball. Place dough in a greased bowl; turn once to grease surface. Cover dough and let rise in a warm place till double (about 1 hour). Meanwhile, combine the ¼ cup margarine and 2 tablespoons sugar; set aside.

■ Punch dough down. Turn out onto a lightly floured surface. Cover; let rest 10 minutes. Roll into a 20x9-inch rectangle. Spread sugar mixture atop. Fold rectangle lengthwise into thirds, forming a 20x3-inch rectangle. Slice crosswise into 96 very thin threads, each ⅛ to ¼ inch wide. For *each* bun, gently stretch a group of 8 threads till they're about 7 inches long. Wrap threads in a spiral around your first 2 fingers, stretching dough slightly. Tuck the end into the top to seal. Place on a lightly greased baking sheet. Repeat with remaining dough. If desired, sprinkle with sesame seed. Cover; let rise in a warm place for 20 minutes. Meanwhile, in a wok place a greased steamer rack over water. Bring water to boiling over high heat. Place buns on the rack so the sides do not touch. (Cover and chill extra buns.) Cover and steam for 10 to 15 minutes or till buns spring back when touched. Repeat with the remaining buns. Serve warm. Makes 12 side-dish servings.

NOTE: Quick-rising active dry yeast is not recommended for this recipe.

Nutrition information per serving: 164 calories, 3 g protein, 26 g carbohydrate, 5 g fat (1 g saturated), 0 mg cholesterol, 101 mg sodium, 45 mg potassium.

炒
鍋
烹
飪

CHINESE SPECIALTY

For a crispy fried version, prepare and shape the **Silver Thread Buns** *as directed. Instead of steaming the buns, in a wok or 3-quart saucepan heat 1½ to 2 inches of cooking oil or shortening to 365°. Fry buns, two or three at a time, in the hot oil for 2 to 3 minutes or till golden brown, turning once. Drain on paper towels. Keep warm in a 300° oven while frying the remaining buns. Serve warm.*

Fold the 20x9-inch dough rectangle lengthwise into thirds, forming a 20x3-inch rectangle. Place the rectangle on a lightly floured cutting board. Starting at 1 end, use a cleaver or sharp knife to cut the rectangle crosswise into thin strips about ⅛ to ¼ inch wide. You should end up with 96 strips of thin dough "threads."

For each bun, gently stretch a group of 8 threads from both ends till they are about 7 inches long. Starting at 1 end, wrap the threads in a spiral around the first 2 fingers of your hand, stretching the dough slightly. Use your thumb to tuck the end into the top of the spiral. At the same time, slide the bun off your fingers onto a lightly greased baking sheet.

PORK BUN FILLING

CHINESE SPECIALTY

This combination of savory pork and vegetables makes a typical Chinese filling for Chinese buns (see dough recipes, pages 138 and 139).

  6 dried mushrooms
  ¼ cup water
  2 tablespoons oyster sauce
1½ teaspoons cornstarch
  1 teaspoon sugar
  1 teaspoon soy sauce
  ¼ teaspoon pepper

  1 tablespoon cooking oil
  1 teaspoon grated gingerroot
  2 green onions, sliced (¼ cup)
  8 ounces lean boneless pork,
      finely chopped
  2 tablespoons chopped bamboo
      shoots

■ Soak mushrooms for 30 minutes in enough warm water to cover. Rinse well; squeeze. Chop finely, discarding stems. Combine the ¼ cup water, oyster sauce, cornstarch, sugar, soy sauce, and pepper; set aside. Pour oil into a wok or large skillet. Preheat over medium-high heat. Stir-fry gingerroot and onions in hot oil for 15 seconds. Remove. Add pork to the wok. Stir-fry for 2 to 3 minutes or till no pink remains. Push from center. Stir oyster sauce mixture. Add to center of wok. Cook and stir till thickened and bubbly. Add mushrooms, onion mixture, and bamboo shoots. Stir all ingredients together. Cook and stir 1 minute more. Makes about 1½ cups filling.

Nutrition information per serving: 47 calories, 4 g protein, 3 g carbohydrate, 3 g fat (1 g saturated), 11 mg cholesterol, 155 mg sodium, 80 mg potassium.

SWEET SESAME SEED FILLING

CHINESE SPECIALTY

For a little variety, next time add ½ teaspoon ground cinnamon to the filling along with the lemon peel.

⅔ cup sesame seed, toasted
⅓ cup margarine or butter,
    softened
¼ cup sugar

2 tablespoons brown sugar
1 teaspoon finely shredded
    lemon peel

■ In a food processor bowl or blender container place sesame seed. Cover and process or blend to a fine powder. Beat margarine with an electric mixer for 30 seconds. Add sugar, brown sugar, and peel. Beat till combined. Add sesame seed powder. Beat till combined. Makes about 1 cup filling.

Nutrition information per serving: 102 calories, 2 g protein, 6 g carbohydrate, 8 g fat (1 g saturated), 0 mg cholesterol, 54 mg sodium, 39 mg potassium.

FOUR-COLOR DUMPLINGS

2 cups all-purpose flour
¼ teaspoon salt
⅔ cup boiling water
3 tablespoons all-purpose flour
3 dried mushrooms
2 ounces fresh **or** frozen peeled
    and deveined shrimp
¼ cup finely chopped water
    chestnuts
2 tablespoons cornstarch
1 green onion, finely chopped

1 tablespoon rice wine
    or dry white wine
1 tablespoon soy sauce
2 teaspoons grated gingerroot
1 teaspoon sesame oil
¼ teaspoon pepper
8 ounces lean ground pork
1 small carrot
1 hard-cooked egg
    Chili Dipping Sauce
    (see recipe, page 112)

CHINESE SPECIALTY
The distinctive garnishing on the tops of these dumplings gives them their name. **(Pictured on pages 130 and 131.)**

■ In a large bowl combine the 2 cups flour and salt. Gradually add boiling water, stirring constantly. Stir in ¼ cup cold *water*. Turn out onto a lightly floured surface; let stand till cool. Knead in enough of the 3 tablespoons flour to make a moderately stiff dough that is smooth and elastic (6 to 8 minutes total). Shape into a ball. Cover and let rest for 20 minutes.

■ Soak mushrooms for 30 minutes in enough warm water to cover. Rinse well; squeeze. Chop finely, discarding stems. Thaw shrimp, if frozen. Chop finely. For filling, combine water chestnuts, cornstarch, onion, rice wine, soy sauce, gingerroot, sesame oil, and pepper. Add pork; mix well.

■ Divide the dough in half. On a lightly floured surface, roll *each* half to a ¹⁄₁₆-inch thickness. Cut into 3-inch rounds, rerolling dough as needed. Spoon 1 slightly rounded teaspoon of filling onto *each* round. Bring opposite sides over filling; pinch together only in center. Pinch remaining sides together only in the center. Repeat with remaining rounds and filling. Enlarge openings atop dumplings. Place on a lightly floured baking sheet; cover. Chill dumplings in the freezer for 20 minutes. Finely chop the carrot and egg. Fill openings with carrot, egg, mushrooms, and shrimp. In a wok place a greased steamer rack over water. Bring water to boiling over high heat. Place dumplings on rack so sides do not touch. (Cover and chill extra dumplings.) Cover and steam about 15 minutes or till no pink remains in pork. Repeat with remaining dumplings. Serve with Chili Dipping Sauce. Makes 10 appetizer servings.

Nutrition information per serving: 173 calories, 10 g protein, 25 g carbohydrate, 3 g fat (1 g saturated), 47 mg cholesterol, 604 mg sodium, 174 mg potassium.

For each dumpling, bring opposite sides of the dough round over the filling. Pinch the dough together only in the center. Bring the remaining sides together, pinching only in the center. Use a chopstick to slightly enlarge the openings atop the dumplings.

HOISIN BEEF DUMPLINGS

CHINESE SPECIALTY

Traditionally, the Chinese prepare and serve dumplings for holidays and festivals, including the Chinese New Year.

2 cups all-purpose flour
⅔ cup boiling water
¼ cup cold water
¼ cup hoisin sauce
1 teaspoon cornstarch

1 cup finely chopped bok choy
2 tablespoons finely chopped
   onion
12 ounces lean ground beef

■ For dough, in a large mixing bowl combine the flour and the boiling water, stirring constantly with a fork or a chopstick. Add the cold water; mix till dough forms a ball (dough will be sticky). Cover and set aside.

■ For the filling, in a large mixing bowl stir together the hoisin sauce and cornstarch. Stir in the bok choy and onion. Add the ground beef; mix well. Set aside.

■ Divide the dough in half. Divide *each* half into 15 balls. On a well-floured surface, roll *each* ball into a 3-inch circle. Shape the filling into 30 balls using about *1 tablespoon* filling for each ball. Place *one* ball of filling in the center of *each* dough circle. Bring the dough up around the filling, pleating the dough firmly, but leaving the top open. Gently flatten the bottoms of dumplings, so they stand upright by themselves.

■ In a wok place a greased steamer rack over water. Bring water to boiling over high heat. Place dumplings, open sides up, on the greased steamer rack so the sides do not touch. (Cover and chill extra dumplings.) Cover and steam for 15 to 17 minutes or till no pink remains in beef. Repeat with remaining dumplings. Makes 10 appetizer servings.

Nutrition information per serving: 178 calories, 11 g protein, 23 g carbohydrate, 4 g fat (2 g saturated), 27 mg cholesterol, 162 mg sodium, 137 mg potassium.

STEAMING VEGETABLES

Ingredients	Quantity	Preparation Directions	Steaming Time
Asparagus	1 pound	Remove tough portion of stems; bias-slice into 1-inch lengths (3 cups) or leave as spears.	5 to 8 minutes
Broccoli	12 ounces	Cut flowerets into bite-size pieces; thinly slice stems crosswise (3 cups).	8 to 12 minutes
Cabbage	Half of a small head	Core and cut into 4 wedges.	10 to 12 minutes
Carrots	4 medium	Thinly bias-slice (2 cups).	8 to 10 minutes
	4 medium	Cut into julienne strips (2 cups).	6 to 8 minutes
Cauliflower	Half of a medium head	Remove leaves and stem. Leave whole or break into flowerets.	8 to 10 minutes
Celery	5 stalks	Slice ½ inch thick.	7 to 10 minutes
Mushrooms	8 ounces	Leave whole or slice.	5 to 7 minutes
Pea Pods	6 to 8 ounces	Remove tips and strings (3 cups).	2 to 4 minutes
Peas	2 pounds	Shell (2 cups).	12 to 15 minutes
Potatoes	1 pound	Peel and cut into quarters, or cube.	20 minutes
Spinach	1 pound	Remove stems.	3 to 5 minutes
Zucchini or Yellow Summer Squash	2 medium	Slice ¼ inch thick (2½ cups).	4 to 6 minutes

Steam up a side dish such as fresh vegetables for dinner tonight. Your wok is the perfect vessel for the job. (See "The Steaming Workshop," page 132.)

■ Prepare the vegetables as directed in the chart. Plan on at least ¾ cup uncooked vegetables for each serving. But you'll want to limit the total amount you steam at one time to about 3 cups. Steaming too many vegetables at once does not allow the steam to circulate freely and can cause uneven cooking.

■ In your wok place a steamer rack over water. Bring the water to boiling over high heat. Arrange the vegetables on the steamer rack. Cover and steam as directed.

■ When the vegetables are done, season them with a little soy sauce, sesame oil, or five-spice powder for an Oriental taste. For a more American flavor, try tossing the vegetables with a little margarine, lemon-pepper seasoning, lemon juice, orange peel, or whatever suits your taste.

Non-Oriental Specialties

Surprise! You can cook more than just Oriental dishes in your wok. In this chapter, you'll find various cuisines represented in our wok-adapted recipes. Here you'll find main dishes, side dishes, and even desserts.

Creamy Salmon and Pasta
(see recipe, page 172)

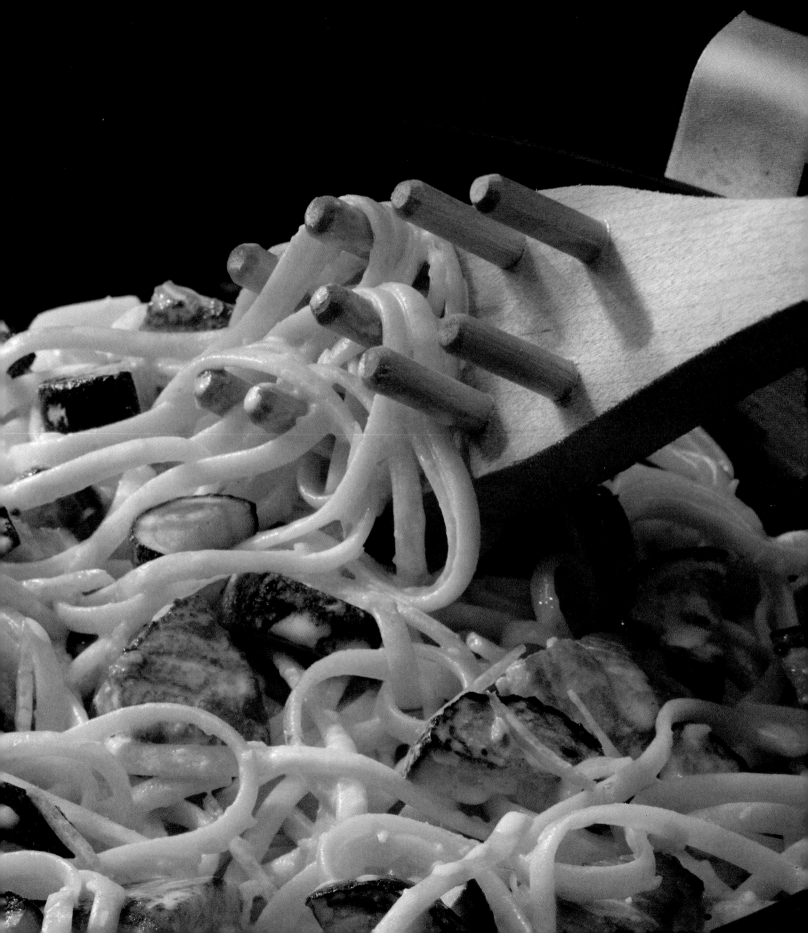

STIR-FRIED STEAK SANDWICHES

Horseradish adds hotness and a pleasant bite to this sauce.

1 pound boneless beef sirloin steak
1 8-ounce can tomato sauce
2 tablespoons steak sauce
1 tablespoon brown sugar
1 to 2 teaspoons prepared horseradish

1 tablespoon cooking oil
1 clove garlic, minced
2 small onions, thinly sliced into rings (⅔ cup)
4 6-inch hoagie rolls, split horizontally
Green pepper rings

■ Trim fat from beef. Partially freeze beef. Thinly slice across the grain into bite-size strips. For sauce, in a small bowl stir together the tomato sauce, steak sauce, brown sugar, and horseradish. Set aside.

■ Pour cooking oil into a wok or large skillet. (Add more oil as necessary during cooking.) Preheat over medium-high heat. Stir-fry garlic in hot oil for 15 seconds. Add the onion; stir-fry about 3 minutes or till tender. Remove the onion from the wok.

■ Add *half* of the beef to the hot wok. Stir-fry for 2 to 3 minutes or to desired doneness. Remove beef from wok. Repeat with remaining beef. Return all beef to the wok. Add the sauce to the wok. Cook and stir till bubbly.

■ Return onion to the wok. Stir ingredients together to coat with sauce. Simmer, uncovered, about 2 minutes or till slightly thickened. Place bottom half of a hoagie roll on each plate. Spoon steak mixture onto bottom half of roll. Top with green pepper rings and top of roll. Makes 4 servings.

Nutrition information per serving: 486 calories, 30 g protein, 56 g carbohydrate, 16 g fat (4 g saturated), 60 mg cholesterol, 958 mg sodium, 658 mg potassium.

BEEF STIR-FRY WITH BLUE CHEESE

1 pound beef top round steak
½ cup dairy sour cream
2 tablespoons all-purpose flour
1 cup beef broth
2 tablespoons crumbled blue cheese
⅛ teaspoon pepper
   Dash ground nutmeg
1 tablespoon cooking oil

2 small zucchini, halved lengthwise and sliced ¼ inch thick (1¾ cups)
2 small yellow summer squash, halved lengthwise and sliced ¼ inch thick (1¾ cups)
4 green onions, bias sliced into 1-inch lengths (¾ cup)
3 cups hot cooked noodles or rice

You can make several versions of this dish. Just omit the sour cream and blue cheese and substitute a sour cream dip with French onion, toasted onion, chive, or bacon and horseradish.

■ Trim fat from beef. Partially freeze beef. Thinly slice across the grain into bite-size strips. For sauce, in a small bowl stir together the sour cream and flour; blend in the beef broth, blue cheese, pepper, and nutmeg. Set aside.

■ Pour cooking oil into a wok or large skillet. (Add more oil as necessary during cooking.) Preheat over medium-high heat. Add zucchini and yellow summer squash; stir-fry for 2 minutes. Add the green onions; stir-fry about 1½ minutes more or till vegetables are crisp-tender. Remove the vegetables from the wok.

■ Add *half* of the beef to the hot wok. Stir-fry for 2 to 3 minutes or to desired doneness. Remove beef from the wok. Repeat with remaining beef. Return all beef to the wok. Push beef from the center of the wok. Stir sauce. Add sauce to the center of the wok. Cook and stir till thickened and bubbly.

■ Return vegetables to the wok. Stir all ingredients together to coat with sauce. Cook and stir about 1 minute more or till heated through. Serve immediately over hot cooked noodles or rice. Makes 4 servings.

Nutrition information per serving: 473 calories, 33 g protein, 41 g carbohydrate, 20 g fat (8 g saturated), 116 mg cholesterol, 325 mg sodium, 731 mg potassium.

BEEF AND CHEESE CHIMICHANGAS

Vary the flavor of these chimichangas by serving them with different accompaniments. Try chopped tomatoes, sliced pitted black olives, guacamole, chives, chopped green onions, or sour cream.

12 ounces beef top round
    or *flank steak*
1 7½-ounce can tomatoes,
    cut up
1 4-ounce can diced green chili
    peppers, drained
2 teaspoons cornstarch
1 teaspoon ground cumin
¼ teaspoon salt
⅛ teaspoon ground red pepper
1 tablespoon cooking oil

2 sliced green onions (¼ cup)
1 cup shredded Monterey Jack
    cheese (4 ounces)
Cooking oil or *shortening*
    for deep-fat frying
8 8-inch flour tortillas
1 12-ounce jar brown gravy
½ cup salsa
Shredded lettuce
Cherry tomatoes
Avocado slices

■ Trim fat from beef. Partially freeze beef. Thinly slice across the grain into bite-size strips. For sauce, in a small bowl stir together the *undrained* tomatoes, green chili peppers, cornstarch, cumin, salt, and red pepper. Set aside. Pour 1 tablespoon cooking oil into a wok or large skillet. Preheat over medium-high heat. Stir-fry green onions in hot oil for 15 seconds. Add the beef to the hot wok. Stir-fry for 2 to 3 minutes or to desired doneness. Push beef from the center of the wok. Stir sauce. Add the sauce to the center of the wok. Cook and stir till thickened and bubbly. Stir all ingredients together to coat with sauce. Cook and stir 1 minute more. Transfer to a bowl; cool slightly. Stir in the cheese. Wipe out wok well. In the wok or a 3-quart saucepan heat 1½ to 2 inches of cooking oil to 365°.

■ Meanwhile, warm the tortillas (see tip, page 159). Spoon about ⅓ *cup* filling into the center of *each* tortilla. Fold in 2 opposite sides. Starting at an unfolded side, roll up each tortilla. Secure with wooden toothpick. Fry filled tortillas, *two* at a time, in the hot oil about 1 minute on each side or till crisp and golden brown. Using a wire strainer or slotted spoon, remove from oil. Drain on a wok rack or on paper towels. Keep chimichangas warm in a 300° oven while frying the others. Meanwhile, in a small saucepan combine the gravy and salsa. Heat till warm. Arrange lettuce on 4 dinner plates. Remove toothpicks from chimichangas. Place chimichangas atop lettuce. Spoon on gravy mixture. Garnish with cherry tomatoes and avocado slices. Serve warm. Makes 4 servings.

Nutrition information per serving: 880 calories, 36 g protein, 57 g carbohydrate, 60 g fat (14 g saturated), 79 mg cholesterol, 1,618 mg sodium, 1,092 mg potassium.

Beef and Cheese Chimichangas

QUICK AND EASY BURGOO

Burgoo, a hearty south-
ern stew of chicken,
beef, and vegetables,
usually takes hours to
prepare. Thanks to
the wok, the use of fro-
zen vegetables, and a
streamlined method, this
burgoo cooks in less
than 30 minutes.

8 ounces beef top round steak
2 medium boneless, skinless
   chicken breast halves
   (6 ounces total)
1 14½-ounce can stewed
   tomatoes, cut up
1 6-ounce can tomato juice
1 tablespoon Worcestershire
   sauce
½ teaspoon sugar
½ teaspoon salt

Several dashes bottled hot
   pepper sauce
1 tablespoon cooking oil
1 10-ounce package frozen
   succotash
½ of a 10-ounce package frozen
   cut okra
¼ cup cold water
2 tablespoons all-purpose flour
   Parsley sprigs (optional)

■ Trim fat from beef. Partially freeze beef. Thinly slice across the grain into bite-size strips. Rinse chicken and pat dry. Cut into ¾-inch pieces. Set aside.

■ In a bowl stir together the stewed tomatoes, tomato juice, Worcestershire sauce, sugar, salt, and hot pepper sauce. Set aside.

■ Pour cooking oil into a wok or large skillet. (Add more oil as necessary during cooking.) Preheat over medium-high heat. Add the beef to the wok. Stir-fry for 2 to 3 minutes or to desired doneness. Remove beef from wok.

■ Add chicken to the wok and stir-fry for 1 to 2 minutes or till chicken is brown. Stir in the tomato mixture. Bring to boiling. Add succotash and okra. Return to boiling; reduce heat. Cover and simmer about 20 minutes or till vegetables are tender, stirring occasionally.

■ Combine the cold water and flour; stir into chicken mixture. Cook and stir till thickened and bubbly. Return the beef to the wok. Cook and stir about 1 minute more or till heated through. Serve immediately in bowls. If desired, garnish with parsley sprigs. Makes 4 servings.

Nutrition information per serving: 293 calories, 27 g protein, 30 g carbohydrate, 9 g fat (2 g saturated), 59 mg cholesterol, 806 mg sodium, 844 mg potassium.

BAVARIAN BEEF STIR-FRY

1 pound beef top round steak
1 12-ounce can beer
2 tablespoons cornstarch
2 teaspoons instant beef
   bouillon granules
¾ teaspoon dried thyme, crushed
4 slices bacon, cut in ½-inch
   pieces
1 tablespoon cooking oil

1 clove garlic, minced
1 10-ounce package frozen
   brussels sprouts, thawed
   and cut in half
1 medium carrot, shredded
   (about ½ cup)
3 cups hot cooked noodles
   or 2⅔ cups hot cooked
   spaetzle
2 tablespoons snipped parsley

The beer in the sauce adds a distinctive flavor to this dish. The stir-fry is equally as tasty when prepared with light beer.

■ Trim fat from beef. Partially freeze beef. Thinly slice across the grain into bite-size strips. For sauce, in a small bowl stir together the beer, cornstarch, beef bouillon granules, and thyme. Set aside.

■ Add the bacon to a wok or large skillet. Stir-fry over medium heat till crisp; remove bacon and discard drippings. Drain bacon on paper towels. Wipe out wok. Pour cooking oil into the wok or skillet. (Add more oil as necessary during cooking.) Preheat over medium-high heat. Stir-fry garlic in hot oil for 15 seconds. Add brussels sprouts; stir-fry about 2 minutes or till brussels sprouts are crisp-tender. Remove the brussels sprouts from the wok.

■ Add *half* of the beef to the hot wok. Stir-fry for 2 to 3 minutes or to desired doneness. Remove beef. Repeat with remaining beef. Return all the beef to the wok. Push beef from the center of the wok. Stir sauce. Add the sauce to the center of the wok. Cook and stir till thickened and bubbly.

■ Return brussels sprouts to the wok. Add carrot. Stir all ingredients together to coat with sauce. Cook and stir about 1 minute more or till heated through. Serve immediately over hot cooked noodles or spaetzle. Sprinkle with bacon and parsley. Makes 4 servings.

Nutrition information per serving: 462 calories, 33 g protein, 44 g carbohydrate, 15 g fat (4 g saturated), 106 mg cholesterol, 653 mg sodium, 689 mg potassium.

STEAMED HAM AND CABBAGE ROLLS

⅓ cup dairy sour cream
2 tablespoons prepared mustard
4 teaspoons cornstarch
1 teaspoon white wine
   Worcestershire sauce
⅛ teaspoon white pepper
1 cup chicken broth

8 large cabbage leaves
2 cups cooked rice
1½ cups diced fully cooked ham
½ cup chopped cabbage
2 green onions, sliced (¼ cup)
1 teaspoon caraway seed

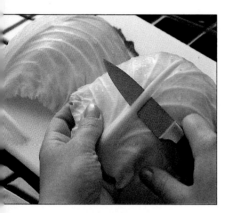

To trim the thick center vein of a cabbage leaf, use a paring knife to carefully cut off the raised portion, keeping the leaf in one piece.

■ For sauce, in a small saucepan stir together the sour cream, mustard, cornstarch, white wine Worcestershire sauce, and white pepper. Gradually stir in the chicken broth. Cook and stir over medium-high heat till thickened and bubbly; cook and stir for 1 minute more. Cover and set aside.

■ Trim center veins of cabbage leaves, keeping each leaf in one piece. In a wok place a greased steamer rack over water. Bring water to boiling over high heat. Place cabbage leaves on the rack. Cover and steam for 4 to 5 minutes or till limp. Remove with tongs, being careful not to break leaves.

■ In a bowl stir together ⅓ cup of the sauce, the rice, ham, chopped cabbage, green onions, and caraway seed. Place about ½ cup of the meat mixture on *each* cabbage leaf; fold in sides. Starting at an unfolded edge, carefully roll up each leaf, making sure folded sides are caught in the roll.

■ In the wok with the greased steamer rack, bring water to boiling over high heat. Place the rolls on the rack. Cover and steam rolls for 20 to 25 minutes or till heated through. With a spatula, transfer the rolls to a serving platter. Reheat the remaining sauce in saucepan and spoon over cabbage rolls. Makes 4 servings.

Nutrition information per serving: 310 calories, 20 g protein, 40 g carbohydrate, 8 g fat (4 g saturated), 38 mg cholesterol, 1,037 mg sodium, 621 mg potassium.

PORK FAJITAS

1 pound lean boneless pork
2 teaspoons chili powder
⅓ cup hot-style vegetable juice
 cocktail
⅓ cup hot-style chunky salsa
1½ teaspoons cornstarch
8 8-inch flour tortillas
1 tablespoon cooking oil
2 cloves garlic, minced
1 large onion, cut into thin
 wedges (1 cup)
1 medium green pepper, cut
 into thin strips (1 cup)

1 medium sweet red or yellow
 pepper, cut into thin strips
 (1 cup)
Assorted toppings (choose
 from shredded cheese; sliced
 green onions; chopped
 tomato; sliced pitted ripe
 olives; frozen avocado dip,
 thawed; or dairy sour
 cream) (optional)

Don't have time to marinate meat for fajitas? We left out that step in making these **Pork Fajitas** *and got delicious results. How? We stir-fried the pork and then quickly cooked it with a flavorful sauce.*

■ Trim fat from pork. Partially freeze pork. Thinly slice across the grain into bite-size strips. Toss pork strips with chili powder. For sauce, in a small bowl stir together the vegetable juice, salsa, and cornstarch. Set aside.

■ Stack tortillas and wrap tightly in foil. Heat in a 350° oven for 10 minutes to soften. Meanwhile, pour cooking oil into a wok or large skillet. (Add more oil as necessary during cooking.) Preheat over medium-high heat. Stir-fry garlic in hot oil for 15 seconds. Add onion; stir-fry for 2 minutes. Add pepper strips and stir-fry about 2 minutes more or till vegetables are crisp-tender. Remove the vegetables from the wok.

■ Add *half* of the pork to the hot wok. Stir-fry for 2 to 3 minutes or till no pink remains. Remove pork from wok. Repeat with remaining pork. Return all pork to the wok. Push pork from the center of the wok. Stir sauce. Add sauce to the center of the wok. Cook and stir till thickened and bubbly.

■ Return the cooked vegetables to the wok. Stir all ingredients together to coat with sauce. Cook and stir about 1 minute more or till heated through. To serve, immediately fill warmed tortillas with pork mixture, then sprinkle with assorted toppings of your choice. Roll up tortillas. Makes 4 servings.

Nutrition information per serving: 509 calories, 29 g protein, 54 g carbohydrate, 21 g fat (6 g saturated), 74 mg cholesterol, 561 mg sodium, 672 mg potassium.

Minestrone

MINESTRONE

12 ounces bulk Italian sausage
¼ cup chopped onion
4 cups water
2 cups loose-pack frozen
    zucchini, carrots,
    cauliflower, lima beans,
    and Italian beans
1 8-ounce can red kidney
    beans, drained

1 tablespoon instant beef
    bouillon granules
1 teaspoon dried basil, crushed
½ teaspoon dried thyme, crushed
⅛ teaspoon pepper
2 ounces spaghetti, broken
1 16-ounce can tomatoes, cut up
    Finely shredded Parmesan
    cheese (optional)

If you wish, choose a different loose-pack frozen vegetable combination that better suits your family's tastes.

■ In a wok or large saucepan cook and stir the sausage and onion over medium-high heat till the meat juices run clear. If necessary, drain off the excess fat.

■ Add the water, frozen vegetables, kidney beans, beef bouillon granules, basil, thyme, and pepper to the sausage and onion mixture. Bring to boiling. Then, stir in the spaghetti. Reduce heat. Cover and simmer about 10 minutes or till the spaghetti is tender, stirring occasionally.

■ Stir the *undrained* tomatoes into the soup mixture. Simmer, uncovered, for 5 minutes more. If desired, sprinkle with Parmesan cheese. Serve immediately. Makes 4 servings.

Nutrition information per serving: 344 calories, 19 g protein, 33 g carbohydrate, 15 g fat (5 g saturated), 44 mg cholesterol, 1,600 mg sodium, 809 mg potassium.

DILLED PORK STROGANOFF

Dill in the creamy sauce makes this pork stroganoff extra special.

1 pound lean boneless pork
¾ cup dairy sour cream
3 tablespoons all-purpose flour
1 cup water
3 tablespoons dry white wine
  or *dry sherry*
1 tablespoon snipped fresh
  dill or *1 teaspoon dried
  dillweed*
2 teaspoons instant beef
  bouillon granules

Dash ground nutmeg
1 tablespoon cooking oil
1 clove garlic, minced
1 medium onion, cut into thin
  wedges (¾ cup)
6 ounces whole small fresh
  mushrooms or *large fresh
  mushrooms, halved*
3 cups hot cooked noodles
  Fresh dill sprigs (optional)

■ Trim fat from pork. Partially freeze pork. Thinly slice across the grain into bite-size strips. For sauce, in a small bowl stir together the sour cream and flour; blend in the water, wine or sherry, fresh dill or dried dillweed, beef bouillon granules, and nutmeg. Set aside.

■ Pour cooking oil into a wok or large skillet. (Add more oil as necessary during cooking.) Preheat over medium-high heat. Stir-fry garlic in hot oil for 15 seconds. Add the onion; stir-fry for 2 minutes. Add the mushrooms; stir-fry about 2 minutes more or till mushrooms are tender. Remove the vegetables from the wok.

■ Add *half* of the pork to the hot wok. Stir-fry for 2 to 3 minutes or till no pink remains. Remove pork from wok. Repeat with remaining pork. Return all pork to the wok. Push pork from the center of the wok. Add the sauce to the center of the wok. Cook and stir till thickened and bubbly.

■ Return the cooked vegetables to the wok. Stir all ingredients together to coat with sauce. Cook and stir about 1 minute more or till heated through. Serve immediately over hot cooked noodles. If desired, garnish with fresh dill sprigs. Makes 4 servings.

Nutrition information per serving: 525 calories, 30 g protein, 41 g carbohydrate, 25 g fat (10 g saturated), 127 mg cholesterol, 554 mg sodium, 613 mg potassium.

PORK AND SPINACH SALAD

12 ounces lean boneless pork
¼ cup white wine vinegar
1 tablespoon sugar
1 teaspoon dried basil, crushed
1 tablespoon cooking oil
3 green onions, sliced (⅓ cup)
8 cups torn spinach
1 cup torn radicchio or
    shredded red cabbage

2 slices crisp-cooked bacon,
    drained and crumbled,
    or 2 tablespoons cooked
    bacon pieces
2 tablespoons grated Parmesan
    cheese
1 cup garlic croutons

If you like spinach salad, you'll enjoy this version. It's enhanced by the addition of stir-fried pork strips and radicchio or red cabbage.

■ Trim fat from pork. Partially freeze the pork. Cut into julienne strips. For sauce, in a small bowl stir together the white wine vinegar, sugar, and basil. Set aside.

■ Pour cooking oil into a wok or large skillet. Preheat over medium-high heat. Stir-fry green onions in hot oil for 1 minute; remove from wok. Add pork to the wok. Stir-fry for 2 to 3 minutes or till no pink remains. Return onions to the wok. Add sauce to the wok. Stir ingredients together to coat with sauce. Cook and stir about 1 minute more or till heated through.

■ In a large salad bowl or serving bowl, combine the spinach and radicchio or red cabbage. Spoon the stir-fry mixture over the spinach-radicchio mixture. Add bacon and Parmesan cheese. Toss lightly to mix. Top salad with croutons. Serve immediately. Makes 4 servings.

Nutrition information per serving: 272 calories, 22 g protein, 15 g carbohydrate, 14 g fat (4 g saturated), 56 mg cholesterol, 333 mg sodium, 949 mg potassium.

WARMING TORTILLAS

For easier rolling, heat tortillas before using. Just wrap a stack of tortillas in foil, then heat in a 350° oven for 10 to 15 minutes. Remove a few at a time, keeping the others warm. To soften tortillas in a microwave, place 4 tortillas between microwave-safe paper towels. Cook on 100% power (high) for 45 to 60 seconds or till softened. Keep the tortillas covered until ready to use.

STIR-FRIED VEAL PICCATA-STYLE

Veal piccata usually consists of veal medaillons fried in butter and served with a wine or lemon sauce. In this veal piccata, the veal is in strips so it can be stir-fried.

1 pound veal leg round steak
   or *lean boneless pork*
⅔ cup water
1 tablespoon cornstarch
1 tablespoon dry sherry
1 tablespoon lemon juice
1½ teaspoons instant chicken
   bouillon granules
1 tablespoon cooking oil
1 clove garlic, minced

1 large onion, sliced
   (about 1 cup)
8 ounces fresh mushrooms,
   sliced (3 cups)
1 medium carrot, shredded
   (½ cup)
3 cups hot cooked spaghetti
   or *linguine*
2 tablespoons snipped parsley

■ Trim fat from veal or pork. Partially freeze veal or pork. Thinly slice across the grain into bite-size strips. For sauce, in a small bowl stir together the water, cornstarch, dry sherry, lemon juice, and chicken bouillon granules. Set aside.

■ Pour oil into a wok or large skillet. (Add more oil as necessary during cooking.) Preheat over medium-high heat. Stir-fry garlic in hot oil for 15 seconds. Add onion; stir-fry for 2 minutes. Add mushrooms; stir-fry for 1 to 2 minutes or till crisp-tender. Remove the vegetables from the wok.

■ Add *half* of the veal or pork to the hot wok. Stir-fry for 2 to 3 minutes or to desired doneness. Remove the meat from the wok. Repeat with the remaining meat. Return all meat to the wok. Push the meat from the center of the wok. Stir sauce. Add the sauce to the center of the wok. Cook and stir till thickened and bubbly.

■ Return the cooked vegetables to the wok. Add the carrot. Stir all ingredients together to coat with sauce. Cook and stir about 1 minute more or till heated through. Serve immediately over hot cooked spaghetti or linguine. Sprinkle with parsley. Makes 4 servings.

Nutrition information per serving: 347 calories, 30 g protein, 40 g carbohydrate, 7 g fat (2 g saturated), 81 mg cholesterol, 403 mg sodium, 691 mg potassium.

LAMB AND LEEK PITAS

12 ounces lean boneless lamb
⅓ cup plain yogurt
¼ cup water
1 tablespoon cornstarch
1 teaspoon Dijon-style mustard
1 teaspoon Worcestershire sauce
¼ teaspoon instant beef bouillon
   granules
¼ teaspoon salt
⅛ teaspoon pepper

1 tablespoon cooking oil
1 clove garlic, minced
1 medium leek, thinly sliced,
   or 1 small onion, sliced
   and separated into rings
   (½ cup)
4 ounces fresh mushrooms,
   sliced (1½ cups)
2 pita bread rounds, halved
   Alfalfa sprouts (optional)

This yummy sandwich may remind you of a Greek-style gyro.

■ Trim fat from lamb. Partially freeze the lamb. Thinly slice across the grain into bite-size strips. For sauce, in a small bowl stir together the yogurt, water, cornstarch, mustard, Worcestershire sauce, beef bouillon granules, salt, and pepper. Set aside.

■ Pour cooking oil into a wok or large skillet. (Add more oil as necessary during cooking.) Preheat over medium-high heat. Stir-fry garlic in hot oil for 15 seconds. Add leek or onion; stir-fry for 2 minutes. Add mushrooms; stir-fry for 1 to 2 minutes more or till vegetables are tender. Remove the vegetables from the wok.

■ Add the lamb to the hot wok. Stir-fry for 2 to 3 minutes or to desired doneness. Push lamb from the center of the wok. Stir sauce. Add the sauce to the center of the wok. Cook and stir till thickened and bubbly. Return the cooked vegetables to the wok. Stir all ingredients together to coat with sauce. Cook and stir about 1 minute more or till heated through.

■ Spoon the lamb mixture into pita bread rounds. Serve immediately. If desired, garnish with alfalfa sprouts. Makes 4 servings.

Nutrition information per serving: 258 calories, 21 g protein, 23 g carbohydrate, 9 g fat (3 g saturated), 52 mg cholesterol, 469 mg sodium, 396 mg potassium.

Vegetable-Stuffed Chicken Rolls

VEGETABLE-STUFFED CHICKEN ROLLS

4 medium boneless, skinless
  chicken breast halves
  (12 ounces total)
2 medium carrots

1 medium sweet yellow, red,
  or green pepper, cut into
  thin strips (1 cup)
1 tablespoon margarine
  or butter, melted
¼ cup orange marmalade

Feature this simple, yet sensational entrée the next time you entertain family and friends.

■ Rinse chicken and pat dry. Place *each* breast half, boned side up, between 2 pieces of clear plastic wrap. Working from the center to the edges, pound lightly with the flat side of a meat mallet to about ¼-inch thickness. Remove plastic wrap. Set chicken aside.

■ Halve the carrots crosswise. Cut each carrot piece lengthwise into quarters. In a medium saucepan cook carrots, covered, in a small amount of boiling water for 2 minutes. Add the pepper strips to the carrots and cook, covered, for 1 minute more. Drain.

■ Brush margarine or butter over the boned side of each chicken piece. Place *one-fourth* of the carrot sticks and pepper strips crosswise onto a short end of *each* chicken piece; roll up jelly-roll style. Secure with wooden toothpicks. Place chicken rolls, seam-side down, in a 9-inch pie plate.

■ In a wok place a steamer rack over water. Bring water to boiling over high heat. Place the pie plate with chicken rolls on the rack. Cover and steam for 8 to 10 minutes or till chicken is tender and no pink remains.

■ Meanwhile, in a small saucepan melt the marmalade. Transfer the chicken rolls to a serving platter. Remove wooden toothpicks. Brush marmalade over chicken rolls. Makes 4 servings.

Nutrition information per serving: 209 calories, 20 g protein, 18 g carbohydrate, 6 g fat (1 g saturated), 54 mg cholesterol, 96 mg sodium, 308 mg potassium.

CHICKEN PICADILLO TOSTADOS

Picadillo (pee-kah-DEE-yoh), a sweet, yet spicy filling, is a favorite in many Spanish-speaking countries. As a tasty alternate, wrap this filling in your favorite kind of taco shell.

4 medium boneless, skinless chicken breast halves (12 ounces total)
1 tablespoon cooking oil
2 cloves garlic, minced
⅓ cup chopped onion
1 7½-ounce can tomatoes, cut up
1 small apple, peeled, cored, and chopped
¼ cup raisins

2 tablespoons canned diced green chili peppers
1 tablespoon red wine vinegar
¼ teaspoon ground cinnamon
¼ teaspoon ground cumin
4 6-inch tostado shells
¾ cup shredded cheddar cheese (3 ounces)
1½ cups shredded lettuce
Dairy sour cream (optional)

■ Rinse chicken and pat dry. Finely chop the chicken. Set aside.

■ Pour the cooking oil into a wok or large skillet. (Add more oil as necessary during cooking.) Preheat over medium-high heat. Stir-fry the garlic in hot oil for 15 seconds. Add the onion; stir-fry for 2 to 3 minutes or till tender. Remove onion from the wok.

■ Add the chicken to the hot wok. Stir-fry for 2 to 3 minutes or till no pink remains. Return the onion to the wok. Carefully stir in the *undrained* tomatoes, apple, raisins, green chili peppers, wine vinegar, cinnamon, and cumin. Bring to boiling; reduce heat. Simmer, uncovered, for 3 to 4 minutes or till half of the liquid has evaporated.

■ To serve, place tostado shells on 4 dinner plates. Spoon about *¾ cup* of the chicken mixture onto *each* tostado shell. Then, layer the cheese, the lettuce, and, if desired, a dollop of sour cream. Makes 4 servings.

Nutrition information per serving: 354 calories, 28 g protein, 27 g carbohydrate, 16 g fat (6 g saturated), 76 mg cholesterol, 379 mg sodium, 503 mg potassium.

PIZZA-STUFFED BUNDLES

12 ounces ground turkey sausage
    or *bulk Italian sausage*
¼ cup chopped onion
¼ cup chopped green pepper
½ cup shredded mozzarella
    cheese (2 ounces)

1 10-ounce package refrigerated
    pizza dough
1 8-ounce can pizza sauce
3 tablespoons grated Parmesan
    cheese

With these stuffed bundles, you get all the flavors of homemade pizza without heating up your oven.

■ For filling, in a wok or large skillet cook the sausage, onion, and green pepper till sausage is brown and vegetables are tender. Drain well and transfer filling to a medium bowl. Stir in the mozzarella cheese. Set aside.

■ Wipe out the wok, if used for cooking sausage. In the wok, place a greased steamer rack over water. Bring water to boiling over high heat.

■ Meanwhile, unroll the pizza dough onto a lightly floured surface. Roll the dough into a 14x10-inch rectangle. Cut into eight 5x3½-inch rectangles. Spoon about ¼ *cup* of the filling onto half of *each* dough rectangle. Moisten edges of dough with water. Fold dough in half over the filling. Seal edges by pressing with the tines of a fork. Place bundles on the steamer rack so the sides do not touch. Cover and steam for 10 to 15 minutes or till bundles spring back when touched.

■ In a small saucepan combine the pizza sauce and Parmesan cheese. Heat over medium heat till warm. Serve as a dipping sauce with the steamed bundles. Makes 4 servings.

Nutrition information per serving: 392 calories, 25 g protein, 38 g carbohydrate, 15 g fat (5 g saturated), 56 mg cholesterol, 1,161 mg sodium, 244 mg potassium.

CACCIATORE-STYLE CHICKEN STIR-FRY

Stir-frying turns this traditionally long-cooking meal into one that cooks in 10 minutes or less.

4 medium boneless, skinless chicken breast halves (12 ounces total), **or 8 chicken thighs, skinned and boned**
1 8-ounce can stewed tomatoes
1 6-ounce can (¾ cup) tomato juice
2 tablespoons dry red wine, (optional)
1 tablespoon cornstarch
1 teaspoon instant chicken bouillon granules

½ teaspoon sugar
½ teaspoon dried basil, crushed
½ teaspoon dried oregano, crushed
1 tablespoon cooking oil
2 small zucchini, sliced (2 cups)
1 2½-ounce jar sliced mushrooms, drained
3 cups hot cooked noodles
2 tablespoons snipped parsley
2 tablespoons grated Parmesan cheese

■ Rinse chicken and pat dry. Cut chicken into bite-size pieces. Set aside.

■ For sauce, in a medium bowl stir together the stewed tomatoes, tomato juice, red wine (if desired), cornstarch, chicken bouillon granules, sugar, basil, and oregano. Set aside.

■ Pour cooking oil into a wok or large skillet. (Add more oil as necessary during cooking.) Preheat over medium-high heat. Add zucchini; stir-fry for 3 to 3½ minutes or till crisp-tender. Remove zucchini from the wok.

■ Add the chicken to the hot wok. Stir-fry for 2 to 3 minutes or till no pink remains. Push the chicken from the center of the wok.

■ Stir sauce. Add the sauce to the center of the wok. Cook and stir till thickened and bubbly. Return zucchini to the wok. Add mushrooms. Stir all ingredients together to coat with sauce. Cook and stir about 1 minute more or till heated through. Toss the noodles with the parsley. Serve chicken mixture over noodles. Sprinkle with Parmesan cheese. Serve immediately. Makes 4 servings.

Nutrition information per serving: 357 calories, 29 g protein, 40 g carbohydrate, 9 g fat (2 g saturated), 93 mg cholesterol, 690 mg sodium, 621 mg potassium.

CHEESY WHITE CHILI

1 tablespoon cooking oil
1 pound ground raw turkey
½ cup chopped onion
½ cup chopped sweet red
   or green pepper
½ cup chopped celery
1 clove garlic, minced
3 cups water
1 15-ounce can great northern
   beans or garbanzo beans,
   drained
1 4-ounce can diced green chili
   peppers, drained

2 teaspoons instant chicken
   bouillon granules
1 teaspoon dried oregano,
   crushed
½ teaspoon ground cumin
¼ teaspoon pepper
¼ cup water
2 tablespoons all-purpose flour
1 cup shredded process Swiss
   cheese or American cheese
   (4 ounces)

This dish looks like navy bean soup, but tastes like mild-flavored chili.

■ Pour the cooking oil into a wok or large saucepan. Preheat over medium-high heat. Add the ground turkey, onion, red or green pepper, celery, and garlic. Cook and stir till the turkey is brown and vegetables are tender. Drain off any excess fat.

■ Add the 3 cups water, beans, chili peppers, chicken bouillon granules, oregano, cumin, and pepper to the meat mixture. Stir till combined. Bring to boiling; reduce heat. Cover and simmer for 30 minutes.

■ In a small bowl stir together the ¼ cup water and the flour. Add the flour mixture to the chili mixture. Cook and stir till slightly thickened and bubbly. Cook and stir for 1 minute more. Add the cheese and stir till melted. Makes 4 servings.

Nutrition information per serving: 432 calories, 34 g protein, 25 g carbohydrate, 22 g fat (8 g saturated), 78 mg cholesterol, 1,174 mg sodium, 720 mg potassium.

TARRAGON-ORANGE CHICKEN

The orange juice and tarragon provide a superb balance of flavor in this fresh-tasting stir-fry.

4 medium boneless, skinless
    chicken breast halves
    (12 ounces total)
    or 12 ounces turkey breast
    tenderloin steaks
⅓ cup water
⅓ cup orange juice
1 tablespoon cornstarch
1 tablespoon honey
1 teaspoon instant chicken
    bouillon granules

¼ teaspoon dried tarragon,
    crushed
1 tablespoon cooking oil
1 pound fresh asparagus, cut
    into 2-inch pieces, **or** one
    10-ounce package frozen
    cut asparagus, thawed
2 medium carrots, thinly bias
    sliced (1 cup)
1½ cups sliced fresh mushrooms
¼ cup sliced green onions
3 cups hot cooked noodles

■ Rinse the chicken or turkey and pat dry. Cut chicken or turkey into thin bite-size strips. Set aside.

■ For sauce, in a small bowl stir together the water, orange juice, cornstarch, honey, chicken bouillon granules, and tarragon. Set aside.

■ Pour cooking oil into a wok or large skillet. (Add more oil as necessary during cooking.) Preheat over medium-high heat. Add asparagus; stir-fry fresh asparagus for 4 to 5 minues or thawed asparagus about 3 minutes or till asparagus is crisp-tender. Remove asparagus from the wok. Add the carrots to the wok; stir-fry for 3 minutes. Add the mushrooms and the green onions the wok; stir-fry for 1 to 2 minutes more or till carrots are crisp-tender. Remove vegetables from the wok.

■ Add the chicken or turkey to the hot wok. Stir-fry for 2 to 3 minutes or till no pink remains. Push chicken from the center of the wok. Stir sauce. Add the sauce to the center of the wok. Cook and stir till thickened and bubbly. Return the cooked vegetables to the wok. Stir all ingredients together to coat with sauce. Cook and stir about 1 minute more or till heated through. Serve immediately over hot cooked noodles. Makes 4 servings.

Nutrition information per serving: 382 calories, 30 g protein, 47 g carbohydrate, 9 g fat (2 g saturated), 91 mg cholesterol, 299 mg sodium, 809 mg potassium.

CAJUN CHICKEN STIR-FRY

4 medium boneless, skinless
   chicken breast halves
   (12 ounces total)
1 16-ounce can tomatoes, cut up
1 tablespoon cornstarch
1 teaspoon instant chicken
   bouillon granules
½ teaspoon sugar
¼ teaspoon pepper
¼ teaspoon ground red pepper
1 tablespoon cooking oil
2 cloves garlic, minced

1 small onion, cut into thin
   wedges
1 stalk celery, bias sliced
   (½ cup)
1 small green pepper, chopped
   (½ cup)
6 ounces smoked turkey
   sausage, halved lengthwise
   and sliced ½ inch thick
2⅔ cups hot cooked grits or
   3 cups hot cooked rice

This dish resembles jambalaya (jam-ba-LIE-ya), a Cajun specialty. The flavor combination of peppery tomato-sauced chicken served with hot grits or rice is common in the southern United States.

■ Rinse chicken and pat dry. Cut chicken into thin bite-size strips. Set aside.

■ For sauce, in a small bowl stir together the *undrained* tomatoes, the cornstarch, chicken bouillon granules, sugar, pepper, and red pepper. Set aside.

■ Pour cooking oil into a wok or large skillet. (Add more oil as necessary during cooking.) Preheat over medium-high heat. Stir-fry garlic in hot oil for 15 seconds. Add the onion and celery; stir-fry for 2 minutes. Add the green pepper; stir-fry for 1½ to 2 minutes more or till vegetables are crisp-tender. Remove the vegetables from the wok.

■ Add the chicken to the hot wok. Stir-fry for 2 to 3 minutes or till no pink remains. Stir in the turkey sausage. Push the meat from the center of the wok. Stir sauce. Add the sauce to the center of the wok. Cook and stir till thickened and bubbly. Return the cooked vegetables to the wok. Stir all ingredients together to coat with sauce. Cover and simmer for 5 minutes. Serve immediately with grits or rice. Makes 4 servings.

Nutrition information per serving: 365 calories, 30 g protein, 32 g carbohydrate, 13 g fat (3 g saturated), 82 mg cholesterol, 801 mg sodium, 627 mg potassium.

Stir-Fried Chicken 'n' Fruit Salad

STIR-FRIED CHICKEN 'N' FRUIT SALAD

4 medium boneless, skinless
  chicken breast halves
  (12 ounces total)
2 medium oranges
  Orange juice
¼ cup chutney, snipped
1 tablespoon salad oil
  or *cooking oil*
1 teaspoon cornstarch
¼ teaspoon curry powder

Dash pepper
4 cups torn romaine or *spinach*
1 medium apple or *pear, cored*
  and coarsely chopped
1 cup cubed honeydew melon
  or *cantaloupe,* or *peeled*
  peach slices
¼ cup coarsely chopped pecans
  or *walnuts*
1 tablespoon cooking oil

For a luncheon, serve this light and refreshing salad with poppy seed muffins or sweet rolls.

■ Rinse chicken and pat dry. Cut into bite-size pieces. Set aside.

■ Peel the oranges. Then, section oranges over a bowl to catch the juices. Add enough additional orange juice to make ¼ *cup.* Set orange sections aside. For sauce, in a small bowl stir together the orange juice, chutney, salad oil or cooking oil, cornstarch, curry powder, and pepper. Set aside.

■ In a salad bowl toss together the orange sections, romaine or spinach, apple or pear, melon or peaches, and pecans or walnuts. Set aside.

■ Pour the 1 tablespoon cooking oil into a wok or large skillet. Preheat over medium-high heat. Add the chicken to the hot wok. Stir-fry for 2 to 3 minutes or till no pink remains. Push chicken from the center of the wok.

■ Stir sauce. Add the sauce to the center of the wok. Cook and stir till thickened and bubbly. Stir ingredients together to coat the chicken with sauce. Cook and stir for 1 minute more. Pour the chicken and sauce mixture over the romaine and fruit mixture. Toss to coat. Serve immediately. Makes 4 servings.

Nutrition information per serving: 351 calories, 22 g protein, 34 g carbohydrate, 15 g fat (2 g saturated), 54 mg cholesterol, 223 mg sodium, 632 mg potassium.

CREAMY SALMON AND PASTA

In a hurry? Speed the preparation time by substituting a 15½-ounce can of salmon, drained, flaked, and skin and bones removed, for the fresh salmon. Gently stir in the canned salmon at the end and cook till heated through. **(Pictured on pages 146 and 147.)**

1 cup light cream
¾ cup grated Parmesan cheese
12 ounces fresh **or** frozen skinless salmon fillets (about ¾ inch thick)
1 tablespoon margarine **or** butter
1 tablespoon olive oil
2 cloves garlic, minced

2 small zucchini, halved lengthwise and sliced ¼ inch thick (2 cups)
3 cups hot cooked linguine
1 teaspoon finely shredded lemon peel
2 teaspoons lemon juice
⅛ teaspoon pepper
Lemon twists (see directions for Citrus Twists, page 200) (optional)

■ Let light cream and Parmesan cheese come to room temperature (allow about 1 hour). Thaw salmon, if frozen. Cut salmon into ¾-inch cubes, discarding bones. Set aside.

■ Place the margarine or butter and the olive oil in a wok or 12-inch skillet. (Add more olive oil as necessary during cooking.) Preheat over medium-high heat till margarine or butter melts.

■ Add the salmon to the hot wok. Stir-fry for 3 to 6 minutes or till salmon flakes easily with a fork, being careful not to break up pieces. Gently remove salmon from the wok. Add garlic; stir-fry for 15 seconds. Add the zucchini; stir-fry about 3½ minutes or till crisp-tender.

■ Reduce heat to low. Add the light cream, Parmesan cheese, cooked linguine, lemon peel, lemon juice, and pepper to the hot wok. Toss gently till linguine is coated. Gently fold in the salmon. Cook for 1 to 2 minutes or till heated through. Transfer to a warm serving dish. Serve immediately. If desired, garnish with lemon twists. Makes 4 servings.

Nutrition information per serving: 496 calories, 30 g protein, 38 g carbohydrate, 25 g fat (9 g saturated), 83 mg cholesterol, 380 mg sodium, 556 mg potassium.

PICANTE FISH

4 4-ounce fresh or frozen
  swordfish, shark, sea bass,
  tuna, monkfish, or cusk
  fillets (¾ inch thick)
1 cup picante sauce or salsa
½ teaspoon dried oregano,
  crushed
1 tablespoon cooking oil

1 small onion, sliced and
  separated into rings
  (½ cup)
4 ounces fresh mushrooms,
  sliced (1½ cups)
1 medium green pepper, cut
  into 1-inch pieces (1 cup)
2 tablespoons grated Parmesan
  cheese

If you want to go for the "burn," heat up this fish dish with hot picante sauce or hot salsa.

■ Thaw fish, if frozen. For sauce, in a small bowl stir together the picante sauce or salsa and oregano. Set aside.

■ In a wok place a steamer rack over water. Bring to boiling over high heat. Place fish fillets in a 9-inch pie plate. Place the pie plate with fish on the rack. Cover and steam for 7 to 9 minutes or till fish flakes easily with a fork. Remove pie plate from the wok. Cover to keep warm. Remove steamer rack and discard water. Wipe out the wok.

■ Pour cooking oil into the wok or a large skillet. (Add more oil as necessary during cooking.) Preheat over medium-high heat. Add onion; stir-fry for 1½ minutes. Add mushrooms and green pepper; stir-fry about 2 minutes more or till vegetables are crisp-tender. Push vegetables from the center of the wok. Add sauce to the center of the wok. Cook and stir till bubbly.

■ Stir all ingredients together to coat with sauce. Cook and stir about 1 minute more or till heated through. To serve, transfer fish to a warm serving platter. Spoon sauce over fish. Sprinkle with Parmesan cheese. Serve immediately. Makes 4 servings.

Nutrition information per serving: 210 calories, 24 g protein, 9 g carbohydrate, 9 g fat (2 g saturated), 45 mg cholesterol, 532 mg sodium, 617 mg potassium.

SALMON WITH HORSERADISH SAUCE

The slight bite of horseradish and the delightful flavor of dill complement the fish in these salmon rolls. (Pictured on pages 194 and 195.)

8 3- to 4-ounce *fresh* or *frozen skinless baby coho salmon, sole,* or *trout fillets*
1 small *sweet red* or *yellow pepper,* cut into 24 thin strips (½ *cup*)
1 small *green pepper,* cut into 24 thin strips (½ *cup*)

Horseradish Dill Sauce
Green or *sweet red pepper stars and moons (see directions for Creative Cutouts, page 194) (optional)*

■ Thaw fish, if frozen. Set aside. In a wok place a steamer rack over water. Bring water to boiling over high heat. Place pepper strips in a 9-inch pie plate. Place the pie plate on the rack. Cover and steam about 2 minutes or till peppers are just crisp-tender. Remove from wok.

■ To assemble, place 3 red or yellow pepper strips and 3 green pepper strips across one end of each fillet. Roll up jelly-roll style. Place rolls, seam side down, in the pie plate.

■ In the wok with the steamer rack, bring water to boiling over high heat. Place the pie plate with salmon rolls on the rack. Cover and steam for 6 to 8 minutes or till fish flakes easily with a fork. To serve, transfer to a platter. Spoon Horseradish Dill Sauce over top of salmon rolls. Serve immediately. If desired, garnish with pepper stars and moons. Makes 4 servings.

HORSERADISH DILL SAUCE: In a small saucepan cook 2 tablespoons sliced *green onion* in 1 tablespoon *margarine or butter* for 1 minute. Blend in 1 tablespoon all-purpose *flour*. Stir in ⅔ cup *light cream or milk*, 1 tablespoon *prepared horseradish*, 1 teaspoon fresh snipped *dill* or ¼ teaspoon dried *dillweed*, and ¼ teaspoon *salt*. Cook and stir over medium heat till thickened and bubbly. Cook and stir for 1 minute more. Makes about 1 cup.

Nutrition information per serving: 252 calories, 25 g protein, 5 g carbohydrate, 14 g fat (5 g saturated), 57 mg cholesterol, 238 mg sodium, 577 mg potassium.

ITALIAN-STYLE SHRIMP AND PASTA

12 ounces fresh or frozen peeled
    and deveined medium
    shrimp
6 ounces linguine or spaghetti,
    broken into 2-inch pieces
2 tablespoons olive oil
4 ounces fresh mushrooms,
    sliced (1½ cups)
1 medium sweet red and/or
    green pepper, cut into thin
    strips (1 cup)

3 tablespoons margarine
    or butter
1 large onion, chopped (1 cup)
3 cloves garlic, minced
¾ cup grated Parmesan cheese
⅛ teaspoon pepper
    Grated Parmesan cheese
    (optional)

Traditional Italian ingredients, including olive oil, mushrooms, peppers, garlic, Parmesan cheese, and pasta, combine with shrimp to make this a winning combination.

■ Thaw shrimp, if frozen. Halve shrimp lengthwise. Set aside. Cook the pasta according to package directions. Drain.

■ Pour the olive oil into a wok or large skillet. Preheat over medium-high heat. Add the mushrooms and red or green pepper strips. Stir-fry for 1 to 2 minutes or till vegetables are crisp-tender. Remove from the wok.

■ Place margarine or butter in the wok. Preheat over medium-high heat. Add the shrimp, onion, and garlic. Stir-fry for 2 to 3 minutes or till shrimp turn pink. Stir in the cooked vegetables, cooked pasta, the ¾ cup Parmesan cheese, and the pepper. Gently toss to mix. Cook and stir about 1 minute or till heated through. Serve immediately. If desired, sprinkle with additional grated Parmesan cheese. Makes 4 servings.

Nutrition information per serving: 457 calories, 27 g protein, 39 g carbohydrate, 22 g fat (6 g saturated), 136 mg cholesterol, 529 mg sodium, 422 mg potassium.

POACHED FISH IN ORANGE SAUCE

This creamy, full-flavored orange sauce isn't full of calories, but certainly tastes rich.

1 pound fresh or frozen skinless flounder, orange roughy, or sole fillets (½ to ¾ inch thick)
1 medium cucumber
1½ teaspoons finely shredded orange peel
1 cup orange juice
1 medium carrot, shredded (½ cup)

1 teaspoon instant chicken bouillon granules
1 tablespoon cornstarch
1 tablespoon water
1 tablespoon vinegar
Orange knots (see directions for Citrus Twists, Loops, and Strips, page 200) (optional)
Fresh basil sprigs (optional)

■ Thaw fish, if frozen. Chop enough of the cucumber to equal ½ *cup*. Thinly slice the remaining cucumber. Set aside.

■ In a wok or large skillet stir together the orange peel, orange juice, carrot, and chicken bouillon granules. Bring the mixture to boiling. Measure the thickness of the fish, then carefully add the fish to the wok. Return the mixture just to boiling; reduce heat. Cover and simmer for 4 to 6 minutes per ½-inch thickness or till fish flakes easily with a fork.

■ Meanwhile, arrange the cucumber slices on a platter. Use a slotted spatula or spoon to place the fish atop the cucumber slices on the platter. Cover with foil to keep warm.

■ Combine the cornstarch and water. Add to the orange mixture in the wok. Cook and stir over medium-high heat till mixture is thickened and bubbly. Cook and stir for 2 minutes more. Remove from heat. Stir in the chopped cucumber and the vinegar. Spoon sauce over fish. Serve immediately. If desired, garnish with orange knots and basil sprigs. Makes 4 servings.

Nutrition information per serving: 132 calories, 18 g protein, 12 g carbohydrate, 1 g fat (0 g saturated), 44 mg cholesterol, 309 mg sodium, 538 mg potassium.

Poached Fish in Orange Sauce

CRISPY-COATED FRENCH FRIES

Cooking oil **or** shortening for deep-fat frying
1 16-ounce package frozen french-fried potatoes, thawed
1 cup all-purpose flour
1 slightly beaten egg
½ cup cold water
½ cup milk
1 tablespoon cooking oil
2 teaspoons ground red pepper
½ teaspoon garlic salt

■ In a wok or 3-quart saucepan heat 1½ to 2 inches of cooking oil or shortening to 365°. Meanwhile, pat potatoes with paper towels to dry thoroughly. For batter, in a medium mixing bowl combine the flour, egg, water, milk, the 1 tablespoon cooking oil, red pepper, and garlic salt. Beat with a rotary beater or whisk till smooth.

■ Dip the potatoes into the batter, swirling to coat. Fry, a few pieces at a time, in the hot oil for 1 to 2 minutes or till golden brown, turning once.

■ Using a wire strainer or slotted spoon, remove fries from oil. Drain on a wok rack or on paper towels.

■ Keep fries warm in a 300° oven while frying remaining potatoes. Serve warm. Makes 4 side-dish servings.

Nutrition information per serving: 780 calories, 11 g protein, 71 g carbohydrate, 52 g fat (10 g saturated), 56 mg cholesterol, 490 mg sodium, 944 mg potassium.

FRUITY BROWN RICE PILAF

    1 tablespoon cooking oil
  ¼ cup chopped celery
  ½ teaspoon grated gingerroot
  ½ cup regular brown rice
1¾ cups water
    1 teaspoon instant chicken
       bouillon granules

  ½ cup chopped nectarines
     or peeled peaches
  ¼ cup raisins
    2 tablespoons chopped walnuts
     or pecans, toasted
  ¼ teaspoon finely shredded
     lemon peel

■ Pour the oil into a wok or medium saucepan. Preheat over medium-high heat. Add celery and gingerroot. Stir-fry 1½ minutes. Add uncooked brown rice. Stir-fry 1 minute more. Carefully stir in water and bouillon granules. Bring to boiling; reduce heat. Cover; simmer 35 to 40 minutes or till rice is tender and liquid is absorbed. Remove from heat. Gently fold in the nectarines, raisins, walnuts, and lemon peel. Makes 4 side-dish servings.

Nutrition information per serving: 183 calories, 3 g protein, 30 g carbohydrate, 7 g fat (1 g saturated), 0 mg cholesterol, 235 mg sodium, 211 mg potassium.

Serve this fruity rice as a delicious accompaniment to poultry.

CONFETTI RICE SUPREME

    2 tablespoons margarine
       or butter
  ½ cup sliced fresh mushrooms
    1 medium carrot, coarsely
       shredded (½ cup)
  ¼ cup thinly sliced green onions

  ¾ cup long grain rice
1½ cups chicken broth
  ¼ cup dry white wine
     or apple juice
  ⅛ teaspoon pepper
1½ cups torn spinach leaves

■ Add margarine to a wok or large skillet. Preheat over medium-high heat till margarine melts. Add mushrooms, carrot, and green onions; stir-fry 30 seconds. Add rice; stir-fry 2 to 3 minutes or till rice is light brown. Add broth, wine, and pepper. Bring to boiling; reduce heat. Cover; simmer 15 minutes or till rice is tender and liquid is absorbed. Stir in spinach. Serves 4.

Nutrition information per serving: 222 calories, 6 g protein, 33 g carbohydrate, 7 g fat (1 g saturated), 0 mg cholesterol, 383 mg sodium, 359 mg potassium.

The colorful vegetables give this pilaf-type rice its festive appearance.

PASTA WITH PESTO PRIMAVERA

Purchase pesto, an Italian sauce made with fresh basil, olive oil, and cheese, in large supermarkets or specialty food shops.

4 ounces packaged linguine
  or fettucine
2 tablespoons margarine
  or butter
2 cloves garlic, minced
2 cups loose-pack frozen
  broccoli, cauliflower, and
  carrots, thawed
1 small onion, cut into thin
  wedges (½ cup)

1 small sweet red or yellow
  pepper, cut into ½-inch
  pieces (¾ cup)
½ cup light cream
¼ cup grated Parmesan cheese
2 tablespoons pesto
2 tablespoons grated Parmesan
  cheese

■ Cook pasta according to package directions; drain.

■ Meanwhile, add margarine or butter to a wok or large skillet. Preheat over medium-high heat till margarine melts. Stir-fry garlic in hot margarine or butter for 15 seconds. Add the thawed vegetables and the onion; stir-fry for 2 minutes. Add the red or yellow pepper and stir-fry about 1½ minutes more or till vegetables are crisp-tender.

■ Add the light cream, the ¼ cup Parmesan cheese, and the pesto. Cook and stir for 1 to 2 minutes or till slightly thickened. Add pasta; toss to mix. Transfer to a warm serving plate. Sprinkle with 2 tablespoons Parmesan cheese. Serve immediately. Makes 4 to 6 side-dish servings.

Nutrition information per serving: 299 calories, 10 g protein, 31 g carbohydrate, 16 g fat (5 g saturated), 18 mg cholesterol, 284 mg sodium, 373 mg potassium.

MACARONI AND LOTS OF CHEESE

1½ cups tricolored corkscrew
    macaroni **or** regular
    corkscrew macaroni
2 tablespoons margarine
    or butter
1 cup sliced fresh mushrooms
    or one 4-ounce jar sliced
    mushrooms, drained
1 green onion, sliced
    (2 tablespoons)

1 tablespoon all-purpose flour
    Dash pepper
1 cup milk
¾ cup shredded sharp cheddar
    cheese (3 ounces)
½ of a 3-ounce package cream
    cheese, cubed and softened
¼ cup grated Parmesan cheese

■ Cook macaroni according to package directions; drain.

■ Meanwhile, place the margarine or butter in a wok or large skillet. Preheat over medium-high heat till margarine melts. Add the fresh mushrooms (if using) and the green onion; stir-fry about 1½ minutes or till vegetables are tender.

■ Stir in the flour and pepper. Add the milk all at once. Cook and stir till thickened and bubbly. Reduce heat. Stir in the cheddar cheese and cream cheese. Cook and stir till cheese is melted. Stir the macaroni and canned mushrooms, if using, into the cheese mixture. Cook, uncovered, for 1 minute. Stir. Sprinkle with Parmesan cheese. Serve immediately. Makes 4 side-dish servings.

Nutrition information per serving: 397 calories, 17 g protein, 39 g carbohydrate, 20 g fat (10 g saturated), 44 mg cholesterol, 359 mg sodium, 212 mg potassium.

Here's macaroni and cheese with a twist. In this cheese lover's delight, tricolored corkscrew pasta is paired with a trio of cheeses—cheddar, cream cheese, and Parmesan.

Sweet 'n' Sour Potato Salad

New potatoes, green beans, bacon, mushrooms, and sun-dried tomatoes make this hot potato salad out of the ordinary.

12 ounces tiny new potatoes, quartered
1 9-ounce package frozen cut green beans
2 slices bacon
1 cup sliced fresh mushrooms
½ cup chopped onion
1 clove garlic, minced
2 tablespoons sugar
1 tablespoon all-purpose flour

½ teaspoon salt
½ teaspoon celery seed
⅛ teaspoon pepper
½ cup water
2 tablespoons white wine vinegar **or** vinegar
1 teaspoon Dijon-style mustard
2 tablespoons finely snipped sun-dried tomatoes (oil pack) (optional)

■ In a covered wok or large saucepan cook the potatoes in boiling, lightly salted water for 12 minutes. Add the frozen green beans; return to boiling. Reduce heat and simmer about 3 minutes more or till vegetables are just tender. Drain; set aside.

■ In the wok or a large skillet cook the bacon over medium heat till crisp. Drain and crumble bacon, reserving drippings in the wok. Set bacon aside. Cook and stir the mushrooms, onion, and garlic in drippings over medium heat till tender. Stir in the sugar, flour, salt, celery seed, and pepper. Blend in the water, white wine vinegar or vinegar, and mustard. Cook and stir till thickened and bubbly. Stir in the potato mixture, bacon, and, if desired, sun-dried tomatoes. Cook for 1 to 2 minutes more or till heated through. Serve immediately. Makes 4 side-dish servings.

Nutrition information per serving: 239 calories, 5 g protein, 37 g carbohydrate, 9 g fat (3 g saturated), 16 mg cholesterol, 445 mg sodium, 553 mg potassium.

LEMONY SWEET WILTED SALAD

6 cups torn sorrel and/or spinach
1 cup peeled jicama cut into
   julienne strips
1 small red onion, thinly sliced
   and separated into rings
   (½ cup)

2 tablespoons honey
½ teaspoon finely shredded
   lemon peel
2 tablespoons lemon juice
¼ teaspoon poppy seed
3 slices bacon, cut up

■ Combine sorrel and/or spinach, jicama, and red onion. In a small bowl stir together the honey, lemon peel, lemon juice, and poppy seed. Set aside. In a wok or large skillet cook bacon over medium heat till crisp. Do not drain. Add honey mixture. Cook and stir till mixture is heated through. Remove from heat. Add sorrel mixture. Toss till coated. Transfer to a serving bowl. Makes 4 side-dish servings.

Nutrition information per serving: 193 calories, 5 g protein, 16 g carbohydrate, 13 g fat (5 g saturated), 24 mg cholesterol, 250 mg sodium, 583 mg potassium.

Sorrel looks almost like spinach, but it has smaller leaves and a sharp, lemony flavor. Keep your eye out for it in the spring, so you can use it in this tasty salad.

LEMON 'N' DILL GREEN BEANS

12 ounces fresh green beans, bias
   sliced into 1-inch pieces
   (2¼ cups)
1 tablespoon margarine or
   butter, softened

½ teaspoon finely shredded
   lemon peel
1 tablespoon lemon juice
¼ teaspoon dried dillweed
1 tablespoon cooking oil
¼ cup slivered almonds

■ In a saucepan precook green beans in a small amount of boiling, salted water for 4 minutes; drain. Stir together margarine, lemon peel, lemon juice, and dillweed. Set aside. Pour oil into a wok or large skillet. Preheat over medium-high heat. Stir-fry almonds in hot oil 30 to 45 seconds or till toasted. Remove almonds. Add green beans to wok; stir-fry 3 minutes or till crisp-tender. Spoon margarine mixture over green beans. Add almonds. Toss till beans are well-coated. Serve immediately. Serves 4.

Nutrition information per serving: 132 calories, 3 g protein, 8 g carbohydrate, 11 g fat (1 g saturated), 0 mg cholesterol, 39 mg sodium, 243 mg potassium.

The fresh green beans in this quick, but elegant side dish keep their color and crispness during stir-frying.

Summer Squash Tortilla Roll-Ups

SUMMER SQUASH TORTILLA ROLL-UPS

6 7-inch flour tortillas
1 tablespoon cooking oil
2 cloves garlic, minced
1 large onion, chopped (1 cup)
1 small zucchini, quartered
    lengthwise and sliced
    ¼ inch thick (1 cup)
1 small yellow summer squash,
    quartered lengthwise and
    sliced ¼ inch thick (¾ cup)
½ of a 4-ounce can diced green
    chili peppers

2 tablespoons margarine
    or butter
2 tablespoons all-purpose flour
1½ teaspoons chili powder
¼ teaspoon salt
⅛ teaspoon pepper
1 cup milk
1 cup shredded Monterey Jack
    cheese (4 ounces)
1 large tomato, chopped
    (1¼ cups)

For a change of pace, try this light-tasting side dish in place of potatoes or pasta.

■ Warm the tortillas (see tip, page 159). Meanwhile, pour cooking oil into a wok or large skillet. Preheat over medium-high heat. Stir-fry garlic in hot oil for 15 seconds. Add onion, zucchini, and yellow squash; stir-fry about 3 minutes or till vegetables are crisp-tender. Stir in the chili peppers. Remove the vegetables from the wok. Cover to keep warm.

■ For sauce, add margarine or butter to the hot wok; heat till margarine melts. Stir in the flour, chili powder, salt, and pepper. Add milk. Cook and stir till thickened and bubbly. Stir in Monterey Jack cheese. Cook and stir till cheese is melted. Stir *one-third* of the sauce into the vegetable mixture.

■ To serve, fill *each* warm tortilla with ⅓ *cup* of the vegetable mixture. Roll up. Top with the remaining sauce and the chopped tomato. Makes 6 side-dish servings.

Nutrition information per serving: 281 calories, 10 g protein, 28 g carbohydrate, 15 g fat (6 g saturated), 20 mg cholesterol, 486 mg sodium, 363 mg potassium.

CHERRY COBBLER

6 *cups fresh* **or** *frozen
unsweetened pitted tart
red cherries*
1 *to 1¼ cups sugar*
¼ *cup water*
4 *teaspoons cornstarch*

⅔ *cup packaged biscuit mix*
¼ *cup chopped pecans*
2 *tablespoons sugar*
¼ *teaspoon ground cinnamon*
3 *tablespoons milk*
1 *pint vanilla ice cream*

■ In a wok or large skillet stir together the cherries, the 1 to 1¼ cups sugar, water, and cornstarch. If cherries are fresh, let mixture stand for 10 minutes; if cherries are frozen, let stand for 20 minutes.

■ Meanwhile, for topping, in a mixing bowl stir together the biscuit mix, pecans, the 2 tablespoons sugar, and cinnamon. Add the milk, then stir just till combined.

■ Cook and stir the cherry mixture over medium-high heat till thickened and bubbly. Spoon topping on top of hot cherry mixture in wok, making 6 mounds. Cover and simmer about 5 minutes or till a wooden toothpick inserted in topping comes out clean.

■ To serve, spoon cherry mixture and topping into 6 dessert dishes. Top with ice cream. Makes 6 servings.

Nutrition information per serving: 401 calories, 5 g protein, 76 g carbohydrate, 10 g fat (3 g saturated), 20 mg cholesterol, 201 mg sodium, 321 mg potassium.

STRAWBERRY-RHUBARB COBBLER: Prepare as above, *except* substitute 4 cups sliced *rhubarb* (about 1¼ pounds) and 2 cups sliced *strawberries* for the cherries.

Nutrition information per serving: 362 calories, 4 g protein, 66 g carbohydrate, 10 g fat (3 g saturated), 20 mg cholesterol, 204 mg sodium, 446 mg potassium.

PEACHES 'N' CREAM BREAD PUDDING

3 cups dry bread cubes
1 16-ounce can peach slices in
   light syrup, drained, or
   1¼ cups frozen
   unsweetened peach slices,
   thawed (cut up any large
   slices)
4 beaten eggs
2 cups light cream

½ cup sugar
2 tablespoons margarine or
   butter, melted
1 teaspoon vanilla
½ teaspoon ground cinnamon
¼ teaspoon ground nutmeg
   Light cream or whipped
   cream (optional)

You can air-dry or oven-dry bread cubes. Spread the cubes in a single layer in a shallow baking pan. To air-dry, cover the pan with a towel. Let the pan stand at room temperature for 8 to 12 hours or till the cubes are dry. To oven-dry, place the pan of bread cubes in a 300° oven for about 15 minutes or till the cubes are dry, stirring several times.

■ In a greased 8x1½-inch round baking dish combine the bread cubes and peaches. In a medium mixing bowl stir together the eggs, the 2 cups light cream, sugar, melted margarine or butter, vanilla, cinnamon, and nutmeg. Pour egg mixture over bread mixture. Cover with foil.

■ In a wok place a steamer rack over water. Bring water to boiling over high heat. Place the baking dish in the center of the rack. Cover the wok and steam for 50 to 55 minutes or till a knife inserted near the center comes out clean. If desired, serve warm with additional light cream or whipped cream. Makes 8 servings.

Nutrition information per serving: 272 calories, 7 g protein, 34 g carbohydrate, 13 g fat (6 g saturated), 129 mg cholesterol, 242 mg sodium, 180 mg potassium.

APPLE-NUT FRITTERS

To vary their flavor, shake these fritters in cinnamon-sugar instead of dusting them with powdered sugar. For cinnamon-sugar, mix ½ cup sugar and 1 teaspoon ground cinnamon.

*Cooking oil or shortening
    for deep-fat frying*
1½ cups all-purpose flour
*⅓ cup chopped walnuts
    or almonds*
¼ cup cornmeal
2 tablespoons sugar
2 teaspoons baking powder
½ teaspoon salt

½ teaspoon ground cinnamon
⅛ teaspoon ground nutmeg
*1 cup finely chopped, peeled
    apple or pear*
1 cup milk
1 beaten egg
*2 tablespoons sifted powdered
    sugar*

■ In a wok or 3-quart saucepan heat 1½ to 2 inches of cooking oil or shortening to 375°.

■ Meanwhile, for batter, in a large mixing bowl stir together the flour, walnuts or almonds, cornmeal, sugar, baking powder, salt, cinnamon, and nutmeg. Add the apple or pear, milk, and egg. Stir just till moistened.

■ Drop batter by tablespoons, 4 or 5 at a time, into hot oil. Fry for 3 to 4 minutes or till golden brown, turning once. Using a wire strainer or slotted spoon, remove fritters from oil. Drain on a wok rack or paper towels. Keep warm in a 300° oven while frying remaining fritters. Serve fritters warm, dusted with powdered sugar. Makes 24 fritters.

Nutrition information per fritter: 102 calories, 2 g protein, 10 g carbohydrate, 6 g fat (1 g saturated), 10 mg cholesterol, 77 mg sodium, 43 mg potassium.

Crunchy Fried Ice Cream

1 pint vanilla, strawberry,
   or chocolate ice cream
2 beaten eggs
½ teaspoon vanilla
2 cups chocolate-flavored crisp
   rice cereal

½ cup shredded coconut
Cooking oil or shortening
   for deep-fat frying
¼ cup whipped cream
¼ cup chopped pecans, toasted

Fried ice cream? This impossible-sounding dessert is easy to make and is sure to impress your family and friends.

■ Scoop the ice cream into 4 round portions. Then place the ice-cream balls in a chilled small metal pan. Freeze about 1 hour or till firm.

■ In a small mixing bowl stir together the eggs and vanilla. Crush cereal slightly. In a 9-inch pie plate stir together the cereal and coconut.

■ Dip each frozen ice-cream ball into the egg mixture, then roll it in the cereal mixture, pressing, if necessary, to coat. Return coated ice-cream balls to metal pan and freeze about 1 hour or till firm. Reserve remaining egg and cereal mixtures.

■ Remove coated ice-cream balls from the freezer. Dip balls in the remaining egg mixture, then roll them in remaining cereal mixture. Return to pan. Cover and freeze at least 1 hour more or till firm.

■ In a wok or 3-quart saucepan heat 1½ to 2 inches of cooking oil or shortening to 365°. Carefully fry the ice-cream balls, 1 or 2 at a time, in hot oil for 15 to 20 seconds or till golden brown, turning once. Using a wire strainer or slotted spoon, remove balls from oil. Drain on paper towels. Then, quickly return the fried ice-cream balls to the freezer. Fry the remaining balls. Serve immediately with whipped cream and toasted pecans. Makes 4 servings.

Nutrition information per serving: 445 calories, 8 g protein, 38 g carbohydrate, 30 g fat (12 g saturated), 156 mg cholesterol, 234 mg sodium, 257 mg potassium.

CURRIED SHRIMP 'N' BROCCOLI BITES

18 large fresh **or** *frozen shrimp*
    in shells
12 to 16 ounces broccoli
½ teaspoon lemon-pepper
    seasoning

2 tablespoons margarine
    or *butter*
1 teaspoon curry powder
½ teaspoon garlic salt
¼ teaspoon paprika
    Dash ground red pepper

If you wish, wrap the shrimp around the broccoli up to a day ahead and refrigerate. Then, brush the shrimp with the margarine mixture and steam them just before serving.

■ Thaw shrimp, if frozen. Peel and devein shrimp. Set aside.

■ Cut the broccoli into 18 flowerets, leaving a 1-inch stem on each floweret (reserve remaining broccoli for another use). Sprinkle with lemon-pepper seasoning. Set aside.

■ In a small saucepan melt the margarine or butter over low heat. Add the curry powder, garlic salt, paprika, and ground red pepper. Cook and stir for 1 minute to blend flavors. Set aside.

■ Wrap 1 shrimp around *each* broccoli stem. Secure both ends of shrimp to broccoli with a wooden toothpick. Brush each shrimp with some of the margarine mixture.

■ In a wok place a steamer rack over water. Bring water to boiling over high heat. Place the shrimp-broccoli pieces on the steamer rack. Cover and steam for 8 to 10 minutes or till broccoli is tender and shrimp turn pink. Using tongs or chopsticks, remove the shrimp-broccoli pieces from the rack. Serve immediately. Makes 18 appetizers.

Nutrition information per appetizer: 31 calories, 4 g protein, 1 g carbohydrate, 2 g fat (0 g saturated), 28 mg cholesterol, 122 mg sodium, 91 mg potassium.

Curried Shrimp 'n' Broccoli Bites

CAJUN CORNMEAL MINIDRUMSTICKS

For a milder flavor, serve these spicy little drumsticks with regular barbecue sauce.

24 chicken wings
   Cooking oil or shortening
     for deep-fat frying
½ cup all-purpose flour
½ cup yellow cornmeal
1 teaspoon baking powder
1 teaspoon onion salt
1 teaspoon dried thyme, crushed
½ teaspoon garlic salt

½ teaspoon ground red pepper
¼ teaspoon white pepper
¼ teaspoon pepper
1 beaten egg
⅔ cup milk
2 tablespoons cooking oil
   Hot-style barbecue sauce
    (optional)

■ For minidrumsticks, flex the large section of each chicken wing back and forth, breaking the cartilage that connects the larger wing portion (the mini-drumstick) with the 2-part wing-tip section. Use a sharp knife to cut through the skin and broken cartilage. (Save the 2-part wing-tip section for stock or soup.) Then use a small knife to cut the cartilage loose from the cut end of each minidrumstick. Remove skin. Push the meat to the top of the bone, shaping it into a compact ball. Set aside.

■ In a wok or 3-quart saucepan heat 1½ to 2 inches of cooking oil to 365°.

■ Meanwhile, for batter, in a medium mixing bowl stir together the flour, cornmeal, baking powder, onion salt, thyme, garlic salt, red pepper, white pepper, and pepper. In a small mixing bowl stir together the egg, milk, and the 2 tablespoons cooking oil. Add the liquid mixture to the dry ingredients. Stir till the batter is smooth.

■ Dip the meaty end of each minidrumstick into the batter. Fry, 3 or 4 at a time, in the hot oil for 3½ to 4 minutes or till batter is golden and no pink remains in the chicken. Using a wire strainer or slotted spoon, remove minidrumsticks from oil. Drain on a wok rack or on paper towels. Keep warm in a 300° oven while frying remaining minidrumsticks.

■ If desired, heat the barbecue sauce over medium-high heat and serve as a dipping sauce with the warm minidrumsticks. Makes 24 appetizers.

Nutrition information per appetizer: 103 calories, 3 g protein, 5 g carbohydrate, 8 g fat (1 g saturated), 17 mg cholesterol, 127 mg sodium, 40 mg potassium.

Use the tip of a sharp knife to cut the cartilage around the bone loose from the cut end of the minidrumstick. Then remove the skin and push the meat of the minidrumstick to the top of the bone, making a compact ball.

CRUNCHY CARAMELIZED CASHEWS

½ cup sugar
2 tablespoons margarine
   or *butter*

½ teaspoon vanilla
8 ounces whole raw cashews
   (1¾ cups)

■ Line a baking sheet with foil. Butter the foil; set aside. In a wok or large skillet combine the sugar, margarine or butter, and vanilla. Cook over medium-high heat, shaking the pan occasionally *(do not stir)*, till the sugar begins to melt. Add the cashews. Reduce heat to low and cook till the sugar is golden brown, stirring occasionally.

■ Pour the cashew mixture onto the prepared baking sheet, spreading out the nuts with a spatula. Cool completely. Break into clusters. Store in a tightly covered container. Makes 6 to 8 appetizer servings.

Nutrition information per serving: 315 calories, 6 g protein, 29 g carbohydrate, 21 g fat (4 g saturated), 0 mg cholesterol, 51 mg sodium, 216 mg potassium.

Looking for a great-tasting food gift? Place these taste-tempting cashews in a decorative tin and give them to someone special.

SWEET-AND-SPICY CEREAL SNACK

½ cup margarine or *butter*
2 teaspoons apple pie spice
   or *pumpkin pie spice*
½ cup sugar
2 cups crispy corn and rice
   cereal

1½ cups bite-size shredded wheat
   biscuits
1½ cups round toasted oat cereal
½ cup raisins or *mixed dried
   fruit bits*

■ Place margarine in a wok or 12-inch skillet. Preheat over medium heat till margarine melts. Stir-fry apple pie spice in hot margarine 15 seconds. Add sugar and stir-fry 30 seconds. Add the corn and rice cereal, shredded wheat biscuits, and toasted oat cereal; stir-fry 3 to 4 minutes or till the cereal is coated and lightly toasted. Remove from heat. Add raisins; toss to mix. Transfer mixture onto foil to cool. Makes 12 appetizer servings.

Nutrition information per serving: 171 calories, 2 g protein, 25 g carbohydrate, 8 g fat (2 g saturated), 0 mg cholesterol, 157 mg sodium, 93 mg potassium.

This crispy, coated, cereal mix is sweet enough to serve as dessert.

garnishes Galore

A simple garnish can turn an everyday meal into something a little more special. You'll find the following six pages loaded with step-by-step directions for making easy yet elegant-looking garnishes.

CREATIVE CUTOUTS
Use a star, moon, heart, or other shape of aspic cutter or hors d'oeuvre cutter to cut shapes from strips of sweet red, orange, yellow, purple, or green pepper. Or, if you wish, peel an orange, lemon, or lime. Then cut shapes from the peel.

Salmon with Horseradish Sauce
(see recipe, page 174)

FLUTED MUSHROOMS

You can make a variety of fluted mushrooms by using any of the following methods. For all three methods, select large, well-rounded mushrooms. Carefully wash the mushrooms and pat them dry using paper towels.

For the first method, hold a mushroom by its stem. Working with the flat side of a sharp paring knife, position the tip near the center of the mushroom and press the knife down to make an indentation. Continue making indentations all around the mushroom, creating a star-like pattern.

This is just one pattern. You can use the tip of the knife to create other patterns as we did.

For the second method, use a punch-type can opener to make a series of *slight* indentations on the mushroom caps in whatever pattern you desire. The number of indentations you can make depends on the size of each mushroom.

For the third method, hold a sharp paring knife at an angle. Then, beginning at the top of each mushroom cap, cut a small wedge ⅛ to ¼ inch deep. Slightly rotate the mushroom and cut another small wedge. Repeat making wedge cuts, spacing them equally around the mushroom cap.

ONION CHRYSANTHEMUMS

Choose small, well-rounded red or white onions. Peel and discard the outer skin of each onion. Leave the root end intact, but cut off any loose roots. Place the onion between two chopsticks or wooden spoon handles on a cutting surface.

Using a sharp paring knife, start at the top of the onion and make a *deep* cut downward toward the root end, stopping at the chopsticks or spoon handles. Continue making deep cuts about ¼ inch apart around the onion. Place cut onion into a bowl of ice water for 1 to 2 hours or till the flower "blooms."

LOTUS FLOWERS

Thinly slice a lotus root. Using a sharp knife, cut out the outer edge of outer holes of each slice to enhance the flower pattern. To tint flowers, place them in cold water tinted with food coloring. Soak until desired color is achieved. Pat flowers dry with paper towels.

EDIBLE FLOWER BOUQUETS

When garnishing food with flowers, select *only* edible flowers. To be edible, flowers must be a nontoxic variety that is free of chemicals. Some favorites are marigold, viola, pansy, nasturtium, chamomile, rose, and rosemary. If you're in doubt about whether a variety or a flower's blossom, stem, or leaf is edible, call your local poison control center or state extension service.

EGG SHREDS

To make egg shreds, pour 1 tablespoon *cooking oil* into a wok or large skillet. Preheat over medium heat. Add 2 beaten *eggs*. Lift and tilt the wok to form a thin sheet of egg. Cook, without stirring, about 2 minutes or till eggs are set.

Slide the egg sheet onto a cutting surface. Let cool. Roll up the egg sheet, jelly-roll style. Then, using a sharp knife, cut the roll crosswise into ⅛-inch-thick slices. Unroll the slices to form egg shreds.

CUCUMBER LOOPS

Select slender cucumbers with few seeds. Cut cucumbers lengthwise in half. Using a spoon, scrape out any seeds. Bias-slice cucumber halves into 1-inch-thick pieces.

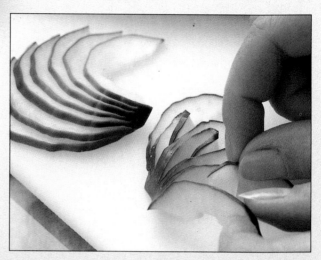

Using a sharp paring knife, cut each 1-inch piece into 7 or 9 bias slices, being sure to leave a narrow spine at one side to hold the slices together. Soak the cucumber pieces in a mixture of 2 cups *water* and 1 tablespoon *salt* about 10 minutes or till pliable.

To form loops, on each cucumber piece start with the second slice and fold it and every other slice in half.

ONION BRUSHES

To make an onion brush, slice off the root end and trim most of the top portion of a green onion. On a cutting surface, hold the onion steady with your fingers. Then, using a sharp paring knife, thinly slash both ends of the onion piece to create fringe. Place the onion piece in a bowl of ice water so the ends will curl back to resemble brushes.

CHILI FLOWERS

Because chili peppers contain volatile oils that can burn your skin and eyes, avoid direct contact with peppers if possible. When working with chili peppers, wear plastic or rubber gloves or work under cold running water. If your bare hands touch the chili pepper, wash your hands and nails well with soap and water.

For chili flowers, select small red, yellow, or green chili peppers. Using a sharp knife, begin at the tip of each pepper and make a cut toward the stem. Continue to make cuts around the chili peppers to form petals. Remove the seeds from the chili peppers. If desired, trim the ends of the petals into points. Then, place the chili peppers in a bowl of ice water so they will open.

TOMATO ROSES

Select red or yellow regular or cherry tomatoes. Cut a base from the stem end of each tomato, but do not sever the peel. Using a sharp, fine-bladed knife, continue peeling each tomato by cutting a continuous narrow strip in a spiral fashion, tapering the end to remove the peel.

Place each strip, flesh-side up, in an S-shape on the cutting surface. Beginning at the end opposite the base, roll up each strip to form a coil or rose shape. If desired, place fresh parsley, basil, or oregano leaves under the base of each tomato rose.

CITRUS TWISTS, LOOPS, AND STRIPS

For citrus twists, use a sharp knife to cut oranges, lemons, or limes into ⅛-inch-thick slices. Then make a cut from the outside edge to the center of each slice. Twist the ends in opposite directions to form a twist.

For citrus loops, use a sharp knife to cut oranges, lemons, or limes into ¼- to ½-inch-thick slices. Cut each slice in half. Then cut between the fruit and the peel, loosening only about three-fourths of the peel from the fruit slice. Leaving peel attached at one end of the slice, fold loosened peel under to form a loop.

For citrus strips, use a vegetable peeler to cut the peel off oranges, lemons, or limes. Scrape any of the white membrane away from the peel. Use a sharp knife to cut the peel into fine strips. If desired, tie the strips into knots or bows.

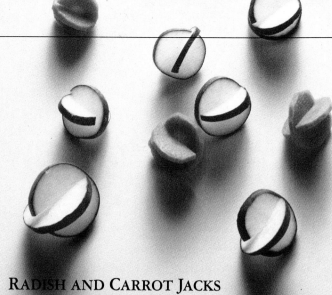

RADISH AND CARROT JACKS

For radish or carrot jacks, use a sharp knife to cut the stem and root from each radish or small carrot. Then cut each radish or carrot into ⅛-inch-thick slices.

Cut a notch from 1 edge to the center of each radish or carrot slice. Soak the slices in a mixture of 2 cups *water* and 1 tablespoon *salt* for 2 to 3 minutes or till slightly pliable. Form jacks by gently pushing 2 slices together at their notches.

ZUCCHINI AND CARROT TWISTS

Use a sharp knife to cut the ends from a zucchini or carrot. Cut the vegetables into 3-inch pieces; then cut pieces lengthwise in half.

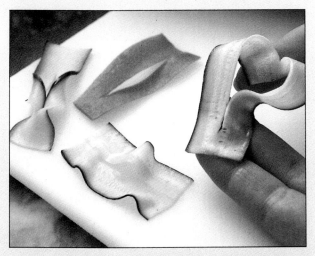

Then, use a vegetable peeler to cut each half into thin rectangular slices. Soak the slices in 2 cups *water* and 1 tablespoon *salt* for 2 to 3 minutes or till pliable. Use a sharp knife to cut a 1½-inch lengthwise slit in the center of each slice. Then fold 1 end of each slice through the slit in the center and pull it straight back. The vegetable will twist naturally.

FRUIT AND VEGETABLE FANS

The basic technique for making fans is the same whether you're using fruits or vegetables. To make fans, use a sharp, fine-bladed knife to cut the fruit or vegetable into thin lengthwise slices, making sure not to cut all the way through the stem end. Then, using your fingers, fan out the fruit or vegetable.

Small fruits such as strawberries, red or green seedless grapes, and kumquats make attractive fruit fans.

For larger fruit fans, try using oranges, lemons, and limes. Cut the fruit lengthwise into quarters. Then slice and fan out each quarter as directed above. For a decorative touch, garnish the tops of fruit fans with mint leaves.

For vegetable fans, choose from a variety of small vegetables. Radishes, cherry tomatoes, small cucumbers, pickled gherkins, baby eggplants, and baby zucchini or yellow summer squash make attractive vegetable garnishes. Some vegetable garnishes, such as radishes, will fan out better if soaked in a mixture of 2 cups *water* and 1 tablespoon *salt* for a few minutes after being sliced.

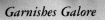

Ingredients

Unfamiliar with an Oriental ingredient? Check this handy ingredient guide before you head for the market. Look for these products at your supermarket, specialty food store, or Oriental grocer. If you can't find an ingredient or prefer to use a more common one, try our suggestions for substitutes.

SAUCES AND FLAVORINGS

CHILI OIL
An oil, flavored with chili peppers, that is used as a seasoning. It adds hotness to dishes. If desired, mix up your own chili oil (see recipe, page 82).

CHILI PASTE
A fiery condiment made with chili peppers, vinegar, and seasonings. Chili paste varies according to the country of its origin. If desired, Oriental chili sauce may be used as a substitute.

COCONUT MILK
A rich-tasting, creamy, white liquid made from the white flesh of the coconut. Coconut milk comes canned in both sweetened and unsweetened varieties. Shake before using.

CURRY PASTE

A combination of herbs and spices ground into a smooth paste. The paste comes in three colors. Red curry paste contains dried red chili peppers, green contains fresh green chilies, and yellow contains turmeric. The flavor varies; yellow paste is the mildest and green the hottest.

FISH SAUCE

A brownish liquid made from salted fish. Its bold, salty fish flavor is used to season foods during cooking and at the table. The clearer and lighter in color the liquid, the more flavorful and better quality the fish sauce will be.

HOISIN SAUCE

A thick, reddish-brown sauce made from soybeans, salt, sugar, garlic, flour, vinegar, and spices. It has a sweet and piquant flavor, and may be used in cooking or as a condiment.

MIRIN

A sweet, syrupy rice wine used mainly in glazes and dipping sauces. Some mirin contains salt and should be used only for cooking. If desired, substitute dry sherry.

OYSTER SAUCE

A thick, brown sauce made from oysters, salt, soy sauce, and seasonings. It has a sweet, salty, fish flavor. Oyster sauce is lighter in color and thicker than soy sauce. Oyster-flavored sauce is interchangeable with oyster sauce in recipes.

PLUM SAUCE

Also called duck sauce. Plum sauce is a thick, reddish-brown, fruity mixture that typically contains plums, apricots, vinegar, and sugar. It is used with appetizers and often is served with meat and poultry. If desired, make your own plum sauce (see recipe, page 82).

RICE VINEGAR

A vinegar made from rice. Rice vinegar has a mild, slightly sweet flavor. Chinese rice vinegars are stronger than Japanese vinegars. If desired, substitute white vinegar.

RICE WINE

A wine that is made from fermented rice and used as a beverage and in cooking. When it is labeled "cooking rice wine," it contains salt and should be used only for cooking, not drinking. If desired, substitute dry white wine.

SESAME OIL

A thick, aromatic, reddish-brown oil, made from toasted sesame seeds, that adds flavor. Because it has a strong flavor, use sesame oil sparingly. You can use it with cooking oil for stir-frying, but never use it alone for frying.

SESAME PASTE

A paste, made from ground toasted sesame seeds, that has the consistency of peanut butter, but the flavor of sesame seeds. In small amounts, peanut butter or other nut butter may be substituted.

SOY SAUCE

A salty brown liquid, made from fermented soybeans, that is used as both an ingredient and a condiment. Soy sauces range in color from light to dark, in taste from sweet and mildly salty to extremely salty, and in consistency from thin to thick. Low-sodium and sodium-reduced soy sauces also are available.

VEGETABLES

BABY SWEET CORN
Miniature corn so tender that it can be eaten cob and all. Buy it frozen, canned, or pickled. Because of its distinct flavor, use pickled sweet corn only when a recipe calls for it.

BAMBOO SHOOTS
Crunchy, ivory-colored vegetables. They come canned, both sliced or whole (cone-shaped). If you buy the cone-shaped shoots, cut the cones into bite-size pieces.

BEAN SPROUTS
Grown from mung beans, sprouts have white stems and yellowish-green caps. Buy them fresh or canned. Fresh sprouts are crunchier. If using fresh sprouts, remove the roots.

BOK CHOY
A Chinese cabbage with long white stalks, dark green leaves, and a mild cabbage flavor. Use both the stalks and leaves in dishes. If desired, substitute regular cabbage.

CHILI PEPPERS
Chilies have smooth-skinned pods and vary in size, flavor, and color. Asian chili peppers may be difficult to locate in the United States. Substitute any of the hot chili peppers that are readily available (see tip, page 27).

CHINESE CABBAGE
Sometimes called Napa or celery cabbage. This elongated cabbage has tightly packed, ruffly leaves with wide stalks, and a mild, sweet flavor. If desired, regular cabbage may be substituted.

PEA PODS
Also known as sugar peas or snow peas. These crisp, green pods have a delicate, sweet flavor. Buy them fresh or frozen. Remove the ends and strings from fresh pea pods before using.

ENOKI MUSHROOMS
Also known as enokitake mushrooms. Enokis have long, slender stems with tiny caps, a delicate flavor, and a crisp texture. Buy fresh or canned. Remove the root ends of fresh enokis.

STRAW MUSHROOMS
Cultivated on rice straw, these brown, umbrella-shaped mushrooms have a mild flavor and a meaty texture. Buy them canned. If desired, substitute another variety of canned mushrooms.

SHIITAKE MUSHROOMS
Large, dark brown mushrooms with thick, meaty caps and a rich, delicate flavor. Only their caps are used. Buy fresh, canned, or dried shiitakes. If desired, substitute other kinds of mushrooms for the fresh or canned forms.

LEMONGRASS
A lemon-flavored grass, resembling a green onion, that is used for flavoring. Buy it fresh or dried. Discard outer layers of fresh lemon-grass before using. Dried lemongrass needs to be removed from dishes before serving.

DAIKON
A large, carrot-shaped, white radish. Daikon is juicy with a mildly spicy, radishlike flavor. If desired, substitute American white radish.

WATER CHESTNUTS
Root vegetables with crisp, white flesh and a mild flavor. Buy them canned or fresh. Canned water chestnuts are peeled, and come whole or sliced. Peel fresh water chestnuts before using.

SEASONINGS AND DRIED PRODUCTS

CILANTRO
Also called fresh coriander or Chinese parsley. It is a flat-leafed parsley with a pungent, almost musky odor that imparts a distinctive flavor to Oriental dishes. Parsley can be substituted for color, but it will not give the same flavor.

FIVE-SPICE POWDER
A seasoning with a pronounced aroma that combines ground star anise, cinnamon, fennel, cloves, and Szechwan pepper. If desired, make your own five-spice powder (see recipe, page 82).

GARLIC
The strongly scented, pungent bulb of a plant related to the onion. Each bulb is composed of small segments called cloves. Besides fresh garlic, you'll find garlic bottled and dried.

GINGERROOT
A knobby root with brown skin and cream-colored flesh. Fresh gingerroot is aromatic with a sharp, spicy flavor. Peel off the skin and then slice or shred the flesh. Ground ginger is the dried version.

STAR ANISE
A dried, star-shaped spice with a licoricelike flavor and aroma. It often comes broken into pieces, but a perfect star anise is an eight-pointed star.

WHOLE SZECHWAN PEPPER
Tiny, reddish-brown berries. If eaten alone, they have a slight numbing effect on the tongue. They lend aromatic flavor to dishes. If desired, substitute whole black peppercorns.

DRIED TANGERINE PEEL

Sometimes called mandarin orange peel. Dark brown and brittle, tangerine peel is sun-dried to produce a pungent-flavored seasoning. If desired, dry your own tangerine or orange peel (see recipe, page 82).

DRIED MUSHROOMS

Also known as dried black mushrooms or winter mushrooms. These edible fungi add a distinctive flavor and a chewy texture to dishes. Different varieties of dried mushrooms vary in appearance, size, and flavor. Soak them in warm water, then rinse and remove the tough stems before using.

DRIED CLOUD AND WOOD EARS

Edible fungi with a brown, wrinkly appearance. Wood ears (also called tree ears) are larger and coarser in texture than cloud ears. Cloud ears are more delicate in flavor. Both are valued for their crispness and rich color. Soak them in warm water, then rinse and remove the tough stems before using. Use cloud and wood ears interchangeably in recipes.

DRIED LILY BUDS

Also known as tiger-lily buds or golden needles. The brownish-gold dried buds add texture and a mild, delicate flavor to Oriental dishes. Soak them in warm water before using.

DRIED RED CHILI PEPPERS

Glossy-skinned, red pods with a hot, fiery flavor. To reduce the hotness, remove the seeds before using. When handling chili peppers, wear gloves to protect your skin from the pepper oils (see tip, page 27).

Cereal and Bean Products

Bean Threads
Also called cellophane noodles. These thin, wispy, dried white strands are made from ground mung beans and are almost transparent when cooked. Except when they will be fried in oil, soften them in warm water before using.

Rice Sticks
Also called rice noodles or rice vermicelli. Made from rice flour, rice sticks are brittle and come in thin, fine strands or as flat noodles. Except when they will be fried in oil, soften rice sticks in warm water before using. If desired, substitute cooked fine egg noodles.

Chinese Egg Noodles
Made from wheat flour, water, and egg. Chinese egg noodles are thin and round or flat. Buy them fresh, steamed, or dried. If desired, substitute fresh or dried fine egg noodles.

Buckwheat Noodles
Also known as soba. These thin dried noodles are made from buckwheat flour. If desired, substitute dried fine egg noodles.

Rice
A seed that comes in several varieties and lengths. *Short grain* rice is round and tends to cling together when cooked, making it good for use in rice cakes or sushi. *Long grain* rice cooks into fluffy, almost separate grains. It is good to serve with stir-fries and other main dishes.

Wonton Wrappers
Squares of noodle dough that are used for making wontons. These wrappers or skins are sold fresh or frozen.

EGG ROLL WRAPPERS
Also called egg roll skins. These square sheets of noodle dough, which are used for making egg rolls, are available fresh or frozen. The thicknesses of egg roll wrappers vary, but the thinner the dough, the flakier the egg roll.

RICE PAPERS
Thin, translucent papery sheets made from rice flour. Rice papers traditionally are used as wrappers for spring rolls, a Vietnamese appetizer.

TOFU
Also known as fresh bean cake or bean curd. A creamy, custardlike product with a mild flavor that is made from soybeans. Buy tofu refrigerated or shelf-stable in consistencies ranging from soft to extra firm. Use firm or extra-firm tofu for stir-frying.

FERMENTED BLACK BEANS
Soybeans that are cooked, fermented in salt brine, and then dried. These pungent, salty beans are used for flavor. Always rinse fermented black beans before using.

BEAN SAUCE
A thick sauce, made from fermented soybeans, that has a salty, full-bodied flavor. It may be made with whole or ground beans, and can vary in color and texture. *Hot bean sauce* contains chili peppers and spices, making it hotter and spicier than ordinary bean sauce.

SWEET RED BEAN PASTE
A thick, reddish-black sauce made from pureed red beans and sugar. It is pleasantly sweet, and is used as a filling for dumplings and desserts.

INDEX

A–B

Keep track of your daily nutrition needs by using the information we provide at the end of each recipe. We've analyzed the nutritional content of each recipe serving for you. When a recipe gives an ingredient substitution, we used the first choice in the analysis. If it makes a range of servings (such as 4 to 6), we used the smallest number. Ingredients listed as optional weren't included in the calculations.

C

Tips and Techniques

Have BETTER HOMES AND
GARDENS® magazine
delivered to your door.
For information, write to:
MR. ROBERT AUSTIN
P.O. BOX 4536
DES MOINES, IA 50336